A CHANCE TO VIEW OUR WAGONS AT REST

As a prospective buyer of railway wagons you'd be lucky to get a close look at one in today's fast moving world of rail freight.

But, at Olympia, British Rail Engineering Limited will be giving you the chance to browse through its selection, at your leisure.

The reposing giant above–the largest modern wagon we have built–will be just one of the stars in our line-up.

There will also be an opportunity to see our latest vehicle–the 44 tonne, 2 axle, Covered Sliding Door Wagon–built to meet the demands of the general merchandise and palletised goods market.

If you want to look at all the specifications we've put them down on paper. But there's no substitute for seeing the real thing. We hope it proves to be an eye-opener.

⇌ British Rail Engineering Limited

Come and see us at London's Olympia Motorail Terminal during the
1981 Private Wagon Exhibition–3rd–7th March 1981, or write for details to;
Commercial Manager, British Rail Engineering Limited, Railway Technical Centre, London Road, Derby, DE2 8UP.

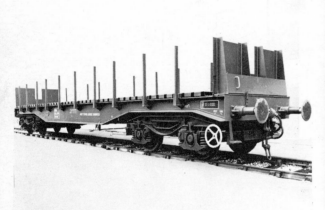

Shell de dum Shell de dum
Shell de dee Shell de dum
Shell de dum Shell de dum
Shell de dee Shell de dum
Shell de dum Shell de dum
Shell de dee Shell de dum
Shell de dum Shell de dum
Shell de dee Shell de dum
Shell de dum Shell de dum
Shell de dee Shell de dum

Music to the ears of railway engineers all over the world. The reassuring hum of diesels purring efficiently mile after mile, year after year, even under the toughest of conditions.

For many years Shell scientists and engineers have developed and track tested lubricants for railroad engines. Because engine life is measured by the performance and protection of lubricating oils, Shell have formulated this range of specialised lubricants for the industry.

Heavy Duty Engine Oils
Shell Caprinus H and Caprinus HP specially designed for General Motors EMD 2-stroke and General Electric 4-stroke diesel engines including use with high sulphur fuels—and oil changes few and far between.

Shell Janus Oils control sludge and piston deposits, minimise wear and still remain filterable and easily monitored.

Bogie Centre Lubricants
Shell Centreplate Lubricant is clean, goes exactly where it's needed and is particularly suited to flat type bogie centres.

Axle-Box Greases
Greases that keep on working as long as they have to, even under the demanding conditions of roller bearing axle-boxes running at high speeds.

Wheel Flange Lubricants
Shell Cardium E.P. Fluids K and J, for use in locomotive-mounted lubricators, reduce wear in wheel flanges and trackside surfaces. Lubricants for trackside lubricators are also available.

Hydraulic Transmission Oils
Shell Tegula Oil 32 successfully meets the complex requirements of transmission systems using hydraulic couplings, torque converters and mechanical gears.

Shell constantly look at ways of improving its range of railroad lubricants. Using its world-wide experience to ensure the products are what the market needs. So every off-duty engineer can sleep peacefully, knowing that Shell keeps 'em running... Shell de dum Shell de dum Shell de dee Shell de dum Shell de dum Shell de dum Shell de dee Shell de dum Shell de dum Shell de dum Shell de dee...

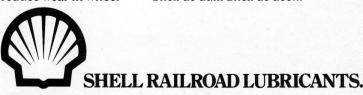

SHELL RAILROAD LUBRICANTS.

PRO

A NATIONW

Procor (UK) Limited

Horbury
Wakefield
West Yorkshire
WF4 5QH

Telephone   Telex
Horbury (0924) 271881   556457 PROCOR G

COR

DE SERVICE

Wagon Repairs Limited

Imperial House
Bournville Lane
Birmingham
B30 1QZ

Telephone   Telex
021-475 5151-7   338758

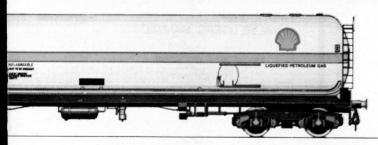

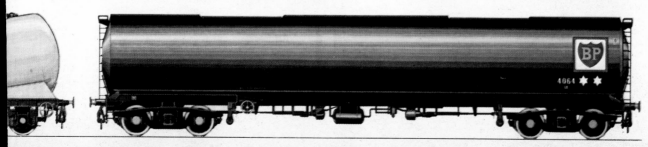

RAIL FREIGHT:
a contribution to the conservation of energy

RAIL FREIGHT:
a contribution to the conservation of energy

I Mech E CONFERENCE PUBLICATIONS 1981–2

Conference sponsored by the
Railway Division of
The Institution of Mechanical Engineers
and The Private Wagon Federation

London 5 March 1981

Published by
Mechanical Engineering Publications Limited
The Institution of Mechanical Engineers
LONDON

Printed by Waveney Print Services Ltd, Beccles, Suffolk
Bound by Mansell (Bookbinders) Ltd, Witham, Essex

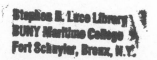

CONTENTS

C32/81

Incentives and opportunities for energy efficiency — an oil company's view

F C KELLY, MSc, PhD and B T HUNTLEY
Shell UK Oil, London

SYNOPSIS   The role that oil will continue to play in the world energy scene is considered, particularly in the light of changes imposed by some major oil producing countries upon the structure
of the international crude oil supply system. Stress is laid upon the potential that exists for
improving the efficiency with which energy can be used and the important contribution that its
conservation can make to the world energy balance. The relative intensities of energy use by the
main freight modes are discussed and their significance in relation to the choice of rail for conveying petroleum products is examined.

THE ENERGY SCENE

During the last 20 years world* demand for
energy more than doubled. Oil met most of this
increase and now provides over half the world's
energy supplies. When we entered this period,
proven reserves of crude oil were, and always
had been, increasing, more oil being discovered
each year than was consumed. But in the late
1960s consumption outstripped discovery, and the
level of world oil reserves began to diminish. At
current levels of consumption existing reserves
would last for another 25 years, and, despite
the finding of oil in such places as the North
Sea and the advances in drilling and production
techniques which allow its exploitation, an
increasing proportion of these reserves as they
are depleted will lie in the Middle East and
other places outside the major areas of consumption. Even now OPEC countries produce less
than 50% of the world's oil, but contain 67% of
its reserves. In contrast there is but 2% of
the world's reserves under the North Sea and
whilst the UK is now enjoying a period of
self-sufficiency, we shall again become a net-
importer of oil by the turn of the century. New
discoveries and enhanced recovery techniques
will add to existing reserves but at the same
time world oil consumption will continue to
increase.

Over the next 20 years it is anticipated
that primary energy demand will grow at about
2% per annum, compared with an average 4% for
each of the last 20 years. But even at this
modest rate, energy demand in the year 2000 will
amount to half as much again as it is now.

New, but conventional, non-oil supplies of
energy take a long time to commission - a new
coal mine might require 7 to 10 years, whilst
a nuclear power station can take 12 to 15 years
to build. Development of unconventional sources
is still in its embryonic stage and will be very
costly to finance.

Thus oil is seen as having to be the
balancing fuel for the next decade, with an
increasing dependence upon the OPEC countries'
comparatively large reserves. Thereafter, oil
consumption will plateau as coal and nuclear
power become greater contributors to the energy
scene and oil usage will be concentrated more on
those purposes for which there are unlikely to
be suitable alternatives.

Security of oil supply

Technically there is no reason why oil
should not meet the increasing world energy
demand well beyond the time that we anticipate
the new dominance of non-oil supplies; oil will
almost certainly be produced and in use in the
year 2100. In addition to the potential of as
yet unexplored oil fields and of enhanced recovery techniques using steam or solvent injec-
tion into existing fields, large quantities of
tar sands and heavy oils in various parts of the
world remain untapped. The Athabasca sands in
Canada for instance are estimated to contain as
much oil as in the whole of the Middle East;
recovery, however, requires special techniques
and is more akin to ore mining with associated
vast amounts of spoil.

But oil production is subject not so much
to technical feasibility as to political
pressures and fiscal programmes of producer
governments. Some countries are deliberately
curtailing their production to conserve their
resources to keep pace with their own economic
development.

During the 1970s the structure of the
international crude oil supply system changed
dramatically as governments of oil producing
countries unilaterally took over numerous oil
concessions previously operated by major oil
companies. Crude oil production over which
governments have complete control rose from 6%
in 1970 to 55% in 1979, and whilst much of this
is still sold to oil companies for distribution
through their integrated systems, OPEC members

---

*Throughout this paper, 'world' refers to world
 outside communist countries.

have also entered into a number of direct government to government sales with the objective of reducing the producing countries' dependence upon multinational oil companies. One of the greatest attributes of a major integrated oil company is its ability to react to, and absorb, the sometimes very substantial fluctuations of the consuming markets whilst maintaining contractual obligations to governments of countries where the oil is produced. This balancing of supply and demand is achieved by a combination of a number of factors including the ability to vary production to some extent, use storage capacity in both producer and consumer countries, vary destinations, and resell to third parties.

Nowadays contracts between producer governments and oil companies are becoming increasingly restrictive and liable to sudden variations. For example, impositions by producer countries either for fiscal or political reasons, or both, may include:

  constraints on volumes and rigid operation of offtakes;

  destination controls;

  prohibition of exchanges or reselling to third parties;

  insistence upon the use of producer country ships.

These factors together with direct government to government sales combine to reduce the flexibility and the cushioning power inherent in the traditional oil trading market. The cost and the availability of crude oil will therefore be very vulnerable to unpredictable factors over which most consumer countries will have little influence. A consumer who has a direct sales agreement becomes even more dependent upon the political whims of its supplier.

Abrupt curtailment of supplies usually, perhaps inevitably, occur in periods of high demand. In both 12 month periods leading up to the October 1973 and the January 1979 crises, world demand for oil was rising. Such crises are not likely to be isolated and further instances could occur at any time. During the next 10 critical years therefore it is essential that we avert, or at least minimise, the effects of any crisis by constraining the demand for oil.

ENERGY CONSERVATION

Whilst much development work is being done within the petroleum industry on alternative energy resources, great emphasis is being laid on energy conservation. For not only is the potential large, in many cases it is realisable within the short term.

Energy can be conserved merely by reducing the quantity and/or the quality of energy consuming activities. But the objective should be conservation by using energy more efficiently without reducing or degrading the end product or service.

Consumption of energy in Western Europe is split roughly 40% domestic, 40% industrial and 20% transport. The potential for improving efficiency is greatest in the domestic sector.

Within industry however it is estimated that by redesigning processes and by integrating energy demands of different processes within individual complexes, savings of 25% could be achieved. Taking an example from the petroleum industry itself, our company has increased the efficiency of fuel usage in its refineries by about 18% over the last 5 years. This figure takes into account the lower level of activity during the period and the savings have been achieved at the same time as upgrading the range of products which the refineries produce. More emphasis has been placed upon 'whitening the barrel', in order to meet the continuously increasing demand for the lighter more 'oil specific' fractions.

Transport

In transport the greatest potential for saving lies in the passenger sector, energy conservation supporting the arguments for greater use of public transport to achieve higher load factors. But as such arguments revolve mainly around non-energy issues, and in any case often depend upon degradation of the service, they will not be debated here.

Setting aside load factors, one study into the potential for more efficient use of energy in Western Europe (ref. 1) estimated that technical improvements for all forms of transport could produce energy efficiency savings of about 25-30%. Rail was seen to have least scope for improvement, and this highlights the premise that rail is already one of the most energy efficient forms of transport. (See Table 1). It therefore supports the oft-quoted argument that traffic should be switched to rail from the higher energy consuming road mode. However, care should be taken not to exaggerate the potential that in practice exists within the UK for such switches and their overall contribution to the saving of primary energy. Road, rail and water serve different markets and tend to complement, rather than compete with, one another. Any substantial shift would occur only as a result of stringent legislation, an unlikely step to be taken by any Government upon energy saving grounds alone since most studies both here and abroad indicate that, apart from trainload movements direct from consignor to consignee, energy consumption incurred in moving railborne traffic is little better than that of road.

A study in 1977 by the Department of Energy (ref. 2) for example, assessed the energy consumption for rail wagon-load traffic as being between 0.6 and 1.7 MJ/tonne/km, and about 1.2 MJ/tonne/km for road transport of comparable traffic. 'Speedlink' services will doubtless operate at the favourable end of the energy range quoted, but there is additional consumption to be taken into account for collection and delivery at either end of the journey. Also allowance should be made for the fact that actual rail distance is often longer than the more direct road haul. Whilst conceding that accurate assessments of energy consumption were extremely difficult to make, the Department concluded that only in the longer term might energy savings accrue from switching to rail and then only if there came about a change in the countrywide pattern of freight movements and distribution arrangements. The study chose technical improvements to vehicle efficiency as the most promising route to fuel conservation.

Table 2 shows the energy consumption of various transport modes as assessed by the Department in its study, and indicates the use made by the petroleum industry of the different modes.

The Incentive Problem

Although energy conservation in the form of fuel economy is generally consistent with cost effectiveness or financial savings, the fuel element cost in most applications, including transport, is low compared with other production costs. In rail the cost of fuel and power represents about 8% of total rail operating expenditure (i.e. costs of train services, including maintenance and depreciation of motive units and rolling stock, track maintenance and signalling expenses) (ref. 3), whilst road fuel costs amount to some 13-15% of total road transport expenditure involved in moving those bulk commodities which are also conveyed by rail.

These comparatively low fuel costs highlight a problem often encountered in investment proposals concerned with energy conservation. In the present climate of economic stringency, industry generally is reluctant to invest in cost saving measures that do not have a quick return of capital, say within 2 to 3 years. Thus, much equipment that was efficient in times of abundant and low cost oil supplies will tend to be retained in service until either it is no longer useful or its life expires. Although in the long term the price of energy will dictate its usage, there is much existing energy consuming infra-structure that is wasteful and inefficient at current levels of fuel costs and availabilities.

British Railways' proposal for increased electrification is possibly a case in point. Although the change is estimated not only to reduce maintenance and operating costs, but also to improve total energy consumption and make the system more independent of oil as a fuel, it is difficult to make a sufficiently attractive financial case with today's criteria of economic evaluation.

For an effective energy conservation programme to be mounted in the shorter term, the investor's view of payback time must be extended by full appreciation of the long term real potential of what has been described as the 'invisible resource' of energy conservation. Briefly this means assessing the capital cost of the conservation measure in unit cost terms over the economic life of the project, and comparing this with the full unit cost of producing the new supplies of energy that would otherwise have to be provided over the same period of time (i.e. including all the costs of mining, manufacturing and distributing).

However, it is recognised that much reluctance will be found in investing capital on 'negative' proposals involving 'invisible' savings, a view which regrettably many consumers take of conservation. In practice therefore it may well be those new developments which were primarily initiated for reasons quite distinct from energy conservation that will prove to be the most fruitful opportunities for exploiting energy efficiency.

OIL BY RAIL

Amongst a number of energy saving developments involving the primary transportation of oil products were the projects in the early 1960s to replace the oil industry's fleets of unfitted tank wagons with wagons built in accordance with the then latest BR design criteria, i.e. maximum payload on 20 ton axles, vacuum braking and 60 mph in loaded and tare condition. The capital cost to the largest UK oil marketing company for refurbishing its fleet in this fashion was some £17 million at the time, or about £130 million in today's money, and substantial additional expenditure was also incurred for the new loading and discharge facilities that were required.

This investment was seen at the time to be financially sound, as indeed it proved to be for many years. At that time the special rates offered by BR for conveyance of products under contract indicated a return of capital in about 10 years, whilst the new rolling stock was anticipated to have a life of some 30 years. Much of the cost effectiveness enjoyed by BR and the industry was due to greater efficiency in which the saving of energy played a large part; for example, the improved pay/gross load ratio of the new wagons, the switching of rail traffic from staged haul wagon-load routes onto block trains travelling directly to their destinations with no intermediate shunting, the predetermined schedules enabling optimum working of locomotives, and the greatly reduced journey time avoiding the need to reheat fuel oil wagons before discharge.

The oil industry's substantial investment in the new rail infra-structure would not have been economic had it not been for the additional traffic that the new-look rail mode attracted. Apart from direct operating cost comparisons with water, road and pipeline, there are probably three other cost related criteria which must be considered - parcel size, reliability and flexibility. The first two are particularly related. In comparison with water or pipeline, rail can provide smaller parcel sizes. Table 3 shows that not only is the total train load comparatively small - not many payloads exceed 1 000 tonnes, the majority far less - but also the individual unit of transportation rarely exceeds 70 tonnes. Thus a train-load can comprise a number of different products without fear of contamination. Small parcels or replenishments mean less working capital tied up in stock. It follows, however, that replenishments must be critically timed if large buffer stocks are to be avoided. Thus reliability of the transport mode is most important. With rail the user may have some doubts about this aspect since, unlike most other modes, he has no direct control over the service.

Flexibility of Rail

Some unease from this point of view may also apply to the other criterion which is probably rail's greatest asset - flexibility.

An integrated oil company with a number of refineries will attempt to satisfy its sales demand over a wide area by the most economic total mix of output from those refineries, each working closest to its optimum. The plants will probably be refining several different types of crude oil, each giving a different yield of refined products, and the production quantities will also vary with the detailed processing routes which are selected.

There are considerable advantages, therefore, in being able to alter the primary distribution pattern to suit the prevailing manufacturing circumstances. Road and pipeline distribution systems for refinery products are relatively inflexible as they are more or less confined to serving given delivery envelopes or specific intermediate depots. Water has a certain flexibility in that planned destinations can be switched at very short notice. It is not uncommon to divert en route a ship to a different destination to that originally nominated in order to relieve a critical stock situation. However, not all water-fed depots can take all the sizes of vessels which are in use for coastal and estuarial distribution in the British Isles, and the long sea hauls involved between east and west coast ports make the flexibility of this mode subject to limitations in practice.

The flexibility that rail offers can therefore be used extensively by consignors to balance their U K refinery production with demand at minimum overall cost.

The new 1960 block train concept involving higher average speeds therefore brought switches from other modes to rail within the oil companies' own distribution networks. Also at that time oil usage was increasing at over 5% per annum and many consumers installed their own block train reception facilities so that oil companies could deliver direct by rail from the refineries. During the 10 years from 1962 UK oil movements by rail rose from 5.2 million to 21.6 million tonnes - an increase of over 300% at a time when country-wide oil consumption rose by only 90%. Since 1973, with falling oil demand, there has been little incentive for existing road fed consumers to install rail reception facilities. The few developments that have occurred include discharge facilities being extended to accommodate larger trains in order to take advantage of maximum trailing loads and so reduce unit freight costs; such schemes are, of course, very compatible with energy efficiency.

Tank Wagons

Reference has been made to the expected life of 30 years of the wagons which were built in the mid 60s. These are still with us and many are, or should be, about half way through their anticipated life. Although we believe BR depreciate their wagons over 15 years, private owners have found little structurally wrong with the vast majority of wagons built in the 60s which could well last a further 10-15 years in normal service.

Had it not been for the reduction in oil demand following the 1973 oil crisis, more high

capacity wagons of 25 ton axle weight and updated suspension design would doubtless have been built in recent years. As it was, although private owners in consultation with BR Engineering and Research introduced high pay/gross load ratio 25 ton axle weight bogie wagons in 1967, few were built in the 1970s. Except for some specialised vehicles for such products as LPG and Bitumen, the market for petroleum products is such that most existing private fleets should be sufficient to carry the anticipated rail-borne trade until they become unfit for service because of fair wear and tear, probably in the 1990s.

However, many wagons are becoming obsolete because of changes in BR design criteria. The decision to change from vacuum to air-braking was unfortunate in its timing in that it meant for many owners changing the specification during the course of a building programme and finishing up with two incompatible fleets. As long as BR retain dual braked locomotives, complete trains of vacuum braked wagons can still be run satisfactorily, but they have to be operated as a separate and isolated fleet thereby reducing the benefits obtainable from full integration.

Such segregation adversely affects the utilisation of wagon fleets by reducing the flexibility which is required by the oil industry. Having fairly specialised wagons with little opportunity for return loads, companies nevertheless operate their fleets to carry as many different products as possible (subject to quality control requirements) and over as many different flows as possible. Thus, essentially the requirement is for a wagon which can convey the widest range of products in combination with all other wagons, and be fully compatible with the loading and discharge facilities at either end of the journey.

Within the oil industry itself there is regrettably a lack of standardisation, various companies having differing wagon lengths, traction couplings and discharge fittings. In our own large fleet however, we see basically only two types of wagon, both of which are operationally compatible and capable of conveying a variety of products. The first type is a Class 'A' 2 or 4 axle vehicle designed to convey Dangerous Goods Classes 3a and 3b but capable of conveying all other 'clean' oil products. The second type is an insulated wagon with internal steam coils designed for carrying all grades of fuel oil, many of which require to be handled at temperatures around 55°C. Even these fuel oil wagons after cleaning can convey 'clean' white oils other than those falling in Dangerous Goods Class 3a. With the current reduction in fuel oil demand, many of these fuel oil wagons are, in fact, being used to carry gas oils and kerosines. Such flexibility again reduces costs by requiring fewer wagons and conserves energy by eliminating shunting and sorting movements.

This flexibility would be enhanced if there were further standardisation of materials and components used in the manufacture of wagons. This aspect is under review by the rail industry, but with the proliferation of different designs which has occurred, the lead time that will be required to obtain any significant degree of standardisation will no doubt be relatively long. The matter is, however, being vigorously pursued at the initiative of the Private Wagon Federation, and close consultation between the technical representatives of British Rail and the various private sector interests has already led to significant progress in formulating recommendations for action in this field.

For some time now the wagon repair industry has been concerned about the reduction in wagon-load services and the problems thus created in moving individual wagons to and from works for repair. Under discussion at present is a proposal by BR to abolish the existing commuted haulage scheme for private owners' wagons and substitute a scheme which reflects more closely the actual mileages run by individual wagons. Such a scheme would certainly have the merit of encouraging energy savings because there would be greater incentives for repairs to be carried out in the field at or nearer the wagons' home base. At least one company has been moving towards this by providing suitable facilities at refineries which will avoid sending wagons to works for statutory brake inspections. The resultant energy saving was not a prime motivator in the decision to install such facilities and is an example of the type of project mentioned earlier where conservation arises from a proposal initiated for other reasons - in this case the principal aim was to reduce the time that wagons due for statutory brake overhaul were out of useful service.

Efficiency - fuel and freight

The oil industry has a keen interest in the continuing development of rail transport both as a user and as a supplier of fuel.

As users we appreciate the flexibility that rail can offer. Also as paying customers we recognise that the comparatively low fuel element in the cost structure of rail transport, and the fact that electrification makes rail less sensitive to sudden variations in oil prices and availability, should assist the rail mode in remaining cost competitive with alternative forms of transport.

As users then, the oil industry has confidence in the role that rail can continue to play in the distribution of oil products and this confidence is demonstrated by some substantial long term investments that are being made at the present time. For example, our company is currently:

- replacing existing hardware at a refinery by completely new rail marshalling and loading facilities capable of handling well over 1 million product tonnes per year;

- constructing new 90 ton 4 axle LPG and 50 ton 2 axle bitumen wagons incorporating many features based upon five years of practical experience with prototypes;

- installing a computer-assisted scheduling system for rail traffic designed to optimise wagon utilisation and loading capacity, which will also have a direct link with British

Rail's TOPS system for monitoring purposes.

Again as users we would like to think that the wealth of technical expertise and pioneering spirit which has led to the development of the Advanced Passenger Train will, in due course, be applied to the development of the rail freight business. In this context, however, we would submit a plea that as far as freight is concerned, high speed over the track should not be regarded as the ultimate achievement. Whilst appreciating the role that higher speeds play in diagramming train paths, our view is that the high speed potential of the freight wagon does not necessarily mean the shortest elapsed time between the two locations which the user considers to be the most important places on the rail network - the orginating point of the consignment and its destination! We are all for high average speed through the system, but we would have less enthusiasm for a system that demanded unduly sophisticated wagon design with high initial and maintenance costs, and high energy consumption, merely to enable freight wagons to make occasional sprints to serve the priorities of passenger services.

As suppliers of fuel - and here it is relevant to point out that many petroleum companies are increasingly concentrating their efforts upon the development of new techniques of producing other forms of energy besides oil - we fully acknowledge the unique role that rail can play in the efficient use of fuel and power. We would therefore encourage the rail industry, in all its diverse applications and uses of energy, to consider carefully the fuel efficiency aspects of any design work that may be embarked upon. Oil is a diminishing resource which in itself increases its real value, and its continued availability for oil specific use in the longer term is of vital concern to the designer, the consumer and the supplier.

References

1. A F Beijdorff 'Energy Efficiency'. Shell International Petroleum Company 1979.

2. Advisory Council on Energy Conservation, Energy Paper No 24 'Freight Transport; Short and Medium Term Considerations' Dept.of Energy 1977.

3. BRB Annual Report and Accounts 1979.

Table 1

Transport – Estimated Potential Savings Resulting From Technical Improvements

	Increase in energy efficiency per cent
Passenger cars	
engine	15
transmission	5
lubricants	5
design – weight, drag, etc.	15
Total	35 *
Ships	
engine	15
drag reduction – anti-fouling, etc.	15
other	5
Total	31 *
Aviation	
engine	15
weight reduction/drag/aerodynamics	10
components	5
Total	27 *
Trucks, Buses	
engine	5
weight	5
deflection foil – drag	5
Total	14 *
Trains Total	10

* Percentage savings are not linearly cumulative.

SOURCE: Energy Efficiency – Shell International Petroleum Company 1979

Table 2

Energy Consumption of Transport Modes and their use in moving Refined Petroleum Products in U.K.

Mode	Energy consumption MJ/tonne/km	Quantity moved per year tonnes x 10^6	Average journey km/tonne
Water – Coastal			
18000 dwt tanker	0.1)	25	470
1000 " "	0.4)		
Rail			
train loads	0.4 – 1.2)	17	130
wagon loads	0.6 – 1.7)		
Road	1.2	49	49
Pipeline (inland)			
36 in dia	0.1)	23	87
8 in dia	0.3)		

SOURCES: DoEn., Energy Paper 24
UK Energy Stats. Table 47. (1976)

NOTES:
1. Tonnage figures exceed total inland deliveries because of double handling.
2. Water movements will include moves to N.Ireland.
3. For all modes except pipeline there will be additional distances travelled by the vehicle/vessel empty or in ballast.

Table 3

Typical parcel sizes of primary transportation modes

Mode	Typical consignment tonnes	Individual product parcel within consignment tonnes	Elapsed time between consignments
Rail	650	minimum 70 or even 30	Extremely variable at consignor's choice, constrained only by ratio of consignment quantity to depot throughput
Water	2000	minimum 400	Constrained only by capacity of reception facility, tidal restrictions and ratio of consignment quantity to depot throughput
Pipeline	Range from 1000 to 15 000 per product		Dependent upon cycle time, e.g. Thames-Mersey line cycle is 10 days.

C35/81

The hirer's role in rail transportation

R W BULL, BTech, CEng, MIMechE
Tiger Railcar Leasing (UK) Limited

SYNOPSIS   The paper reviews the benefits of the lease/hire provision of railcars together with the 'economies of scale' available in the lease/hire route. It suggests that wagon hirers must be innovative and the structure of a rail based distribution system involving private investment is illustrated. The impact of energy costs on rail freight charges should be analysed and reflected in charges for hauling the more efficient wagons which would apply to the ROADRAILER currently being developed in America.

A brief review of current major transportation issues could be summarised as follows:

a)   It is in the best interests of the citizens of a nation to foster transportation services of such efficiency as to consume the minimum of that nations energy and labour resources.

b)   It is in the best interests of that nation's shippers to adopt equipment, technology and operating practises which are the most economic of the various transportation modes and which can be readily marketed by the shipper to his public at adequate profit levels and sufficient for the survival of the supplier of transportation.

c)   It is in the best interest of a nation's railway freight system to provide a comprehensive service recognising that the transportation of manufactured goods and merchandise frequently involves a combination of rail and road between origin and destination.

It is in the area of equipment supply that the hirer has played a traditional role, but as will be seen later in this paper, the hirer of railway equipment must take cognizance of these factors, take commercial initiatives and promote technological developments to ensure that railfreight transportation remains ahead of its competition.

The wagon hiring industry, contrary to popular belief and the image the industry tends to project, is not new. The Birmingham Wagon Company was constituted on 20th March 1885 (1) , and within 7 years a further 18 wagon companies had emerged including the North Central Wagon Company later to become known as Lombard North Central. By 1867 the North Central Wagon Company had a fleet of approximately 3500 wagons.

By far the majority of the 18 600 wagons currently operated by private companies on British Railways are financed either by hire or lease. The principle reasons for this is because hiring/leasing:

Is an additional source of finance to conventional financing techniques

Avoids constraints of the 'gearing ratio' of equity and debt

Provides fixed rate finance and thus predictable costs

Is external to users balance sheet

Is extremely competitive to traditional financing

Gives inflation protection to the equipment

Has a low administration cost

Is self financing as payments are made from the revenue/cost saving generated by the equipment

Enhances cash flow

These factors apply in the case of any equipment acquired by conventional leasing techniques and with railway equipment additional benefits are realised by the end user.

a) Finance provided by specialists who understand wagon technology and operating criteria

b) Specific types of wagon can be provided on a 'spot' basis

c) Wagons are often manufactured on a speculative basis and in anticipation of demand

d) Full maintenance/administration services are provided by the wagon hiring company

e) Wagons must conform with statutory requirements for safety, operation and product integrity, changes in which must be closely monitored to ensure regulatory compliance.

Most hirers operate a fleet of considerable size but whose wagons may be employed
by a large number of small users. It is thus
possible for the small user to benefit from
the 'economies of scale' of bulk purchases of
new wagons and the provision of maintenance/
administration services by the hirer spread
over the total fleet. If such services were
not available, the cost to the end user to
purchase and effectively operate a minimum
fleet would probably result in uneconomic
rail transportation of the end product.

It should be remembered that the wagon
hirer is a specialist in the design of
railcars and he therefore provides, in his
opinion, the optimum design of wagon to meet
the requirements of the customer. It is the
differentiation of design, quality of service
amd costs that separate one hirer from
another.

Whilst users are specialists in their
particular product technology, they frequently
require guidance on those parts of cars which
have no contact with the product, e.g.
running gear, braking systems etc. Whilst
the industry is now endeavouring to standardise on component equipment, this is a recent
development only affecting new cars, and the
cost of hitherto absence of policy is now
being experienced by the owner. Time served
operating experience on wagons dictates that
a new component or novel feature of a wagon
should be throughly tested and proven before
being implemented as a 'standard' in the
name of 'progress'. Twenty years of rapid
'progress' is now being felt in maintenance
expense by owners. Two-axled wagons currently
dominate the wagon scene, but the economics
and acceptability of the four-axled wagon is
rapidly becoming obvious and will, I believe,
become a feature of the Industry in the next
decade. The superior economics of first cost
and payload/tare ratio of the four-axled
wagon are well-known, but exponents of the
smaller two-axled variety frequently allege
that 'down-time' is a minimum with two-axled
wagons and explain its preponderance. The
experiences of my own company both in the UK,
Western Europe, North America, Canada and
Mexico show this to be a fallacy. Wagon
productivity is a function of availability
(after maintenance and repair) and the
operational capability of the railway system
on which it operates. Whilst the former can
be compared on an International basis,
statistics on railway efficiency are more
difficult to compare due to interpretation and
the mix of traffic. For example, whilst
BR's load factor is substantially higher
than those of other Western European railways,
this disguises the fact that BR's average
wagon capacity is the lowest in Europe even
though the maximum allowable axleload is
28% higher.

With deregulation of railways in North
America and the quest for an increased market
share by the railways of Western Europe, I
believe that the role of the hirer will
change to complement the rationalisation
policy of railways and evidenced as being

desirable in the name of efficiency and
energy conservation expounded at the
beginning of this paper. To this end, the
private sector in the railway industry must
accept the challenges afforded by this
rationalisation and become in themselves
transportation agencies, providing a total
distribution system and accepting the attend-
ant operational risks.

There is no such thing as an 'ideal' or
model rail distribution system for freight
which can be used to convince an often
sceptical marketplace of its virtues. The
lessons of aggregates cannot be related to
cans of soup any more than coal can be
compared to reels of paper. Let us try then
to define the systems. Firstly there is that
of true bulk catering for the movement of
raw materials or semi-finished products from
place of extraction or manufacture to the
place of processing or completion. Secondly
there is the movement of finished products
to the point of sale.

The first group takes us into the area
of train load movements from private siding
to private siding, often in the form of inter-
works movements whilst the second takes us
from factory to the warehouse or supermarket
and calls for the transport operator to
concern himself with the single pallet.
These are the two extremes of distribution
and whilst there are areas of common ground,
I should like to deal with them separately.

The train moving from private siding to
private siding, increasingly composed of
privately owned wagons, is an extension of
the industrial production line running to a
timetable and giving the highest utilisation
of the physical assets employed. The wagons
forming the train are custom designed for the
products involved to facilitate maximum payload, rapid loading and discharge. Similarly
the terminals are complete intensive specialised installations.

The movement of finished products to
point of sale is an area in which the railways were, not so long ago, almost prepared
to throw their hand in. Elderly rolling
stock, marshalling yards, erratic transits
and antiquated terminals contributed to
the decline of this business in the face of
the motorway and the lorry. But a revolution
has taken place which is changing the picture
completely.

Firstly there is the assault on the
lorry itself, the rising price of fuel,
legislation on tachographs and drivers' hours,
the realisation that motorways are not the
universal panacea we thought and the growing
voice of the environmental lobby. Secondly
and simultaneously, have come the changes in
railway practice, the move to airbraking,
the adoption of the Speedlink concept and
the introduction of TOPS. These changes and
innovations have created a new climate in
which industry has been prepared to look
again at a wagon load rail service.

© IMechE 1981   C35/81

However, we cannot sell, lease or employ wagons without proper regard to their compatibility with the rest of the distribution chain. Therefore we have to be prepared to listen, advise and participate in the total planning process and at a time when more and more industrialists are saying that their job is to produce 'x' and not transport it is surely our role to produce 'transport' and give the service that a road operator offers.

This then is the real revolution in the wagon load business, so let us take two products as illustrations of the systems required.

Our first product is granulated and is required at the point of consumption in 20 tonne lots, so we need:

a) A pressure differential railcar, and we have to determine with the forwarder the requirements of his production line – do we need a 20 tonne capacity wagon to discharge direct to a 20 tonne road vehicle or are there benefits to have a higher capacity car discharging to intermediate silos at the railhead? And if we recommend silos what steps must we or our agents take to prevent contamination or degradation.

b) Having resolved the physical problems then we must concern ourselves with the terms of sale, is the producer to sell 'ex works', 'free on rail' or 'delivered' and once these questions are resolved we may well find ourselves with contractual obligations, product and wagon insurance, documentation and invoicing, and where cross-channel traffics are involved, customs formalities.

These responsibilities are a far cry from the traditional hire and leasing of railcars but an essential part of a total transportation package.

The situation is further complicated in our second example, for here the producer manufactures cans of foodstuffs produced on pallets and his customer required delivery of single pallets and, being a supermarket, has specific days and times for acceptance.

Therefore to all the ramificaions of bulk movement in terms of railcar design we may be certain the producer will wish to sell on a delivered basis and will have no interest in a rail 'package' if this service is not offered. Therefore a railcar carrying pallets to a distribution point will not provide the store until final delivery is required so we need a transit store, perhaps even a warehouse to hold a strategic stockpile, (which if the goods are perishable needs a 'turnover' control), and an administration to arrange the booking in of deliveries and the organisation of the loading of the road vehicles to ensure the most economic local distribution patterns.

Use of the word 'economic' of course reminds me that however efficient, environmentally desirable and technologically brilliant on rail orientated distribution package may be then if it is not financially competitive when compared with the alternative modes of transport then the planning exercise will remain just that.

My own company's experience of being a customer of the railways is that the rate quoted for the job is ultimately economic for the rail portion of the product's journey, provided that rehandling and road redistribution is understated in the equation. It is expertise in this area that renders an inter modal transportation commercially viable. Meanwhile the energy contribution in the rail freight is significantly less than in road haulage and this inherent advantage is being capitalised upon by my parent company in the U.S.A. who have developed the ROADRAILER (figure 1). Although considered uneconomic in the U.K. during the 1960s, with some development, this system is now a viable, commercial proposition and compares very favourably with competitive means of transportation as witnessed in Table 1.

In the face of such developments it is with confidence that I forecast that British Rail will play an increasing role in freight transportation in the next decade, and probably more so than their own tonne-kilometre projections suggest. However, the national railway system will need to be sufficiently flexible to accept the changing and challenging demands imposed upon it by the freighting industry. This railway will probably be the most highly financed by the private sector, than has existed since nationalisation.

REFERENCE

(1) CLARK T.M. 'Leasing' Chapter 1, page 6.

(2) BRITISH RAILWAYS BOARD 'European Railways Performance Comparisions'

Table 1

Feature compared with ROADRAILER	Kangaroo System	Container System
Higher in weight	178%	110%
Higher in equipment first cost	46%	24%
Higher terminal investment	39%	39%
Higher in energy consumption	78%	57%
Higher variable costs	38%	26%

Fig 1   Prototype Roadrailers under commissioning trials at 170 mile/h

C33/81

Railfreight international; the train ferry revival

J A C EVANS
British Railways

At the time when the railfreight business is under siege - hard hit in 1980 by the steel strike at the beginning of the year and by the general recession in the economy - it may seem not a little unusual that part of that same business is working round the clock to cope with the traffic it has, is expanding capacity, and is successfully competing in the market place, aiming to nearly triple its tonnage by 1985. And yet this is the case of the international freight business within BR today.

INTRODUCTION

Railways - as a developed and practical means of through surface transport - have existed for about 100 years, although they began about 50 years earlier. Born in Britain, at a time when the level of technological achievement was inadequate for surmounting all the natural obstacles in their path, they developed in isolated sections, with no logical and unified system. Britain, of course, was isolated on the edge of Europe, and development, earlier and more rapid, was not always in line with the rest - a situation which still gives us some of the special problems we face in international traffic today, such as our restricted loading guage. In the latter part of the 19th century though, moves to co-opera-tion and the development of true international rail services began, and co-ordinating bodies emerged to set standards in particular fields. The first major impetus was the Franco Prussian War of 1871. It was the first European War to involve major troop movements by rail, and the united Germany that followed caused the rail-ways of the separate German Kingdoms to be linked together quickly. In the 43 peaceful years that followed, the true foundations of international rail co-operation were laid.

The Conference for Technical Unity in 1882 established the common loading gauge - known as Berne Gauge - which now applied throughout main-land Europe. In 1890, the International Convention concerning the Carriage of Goods, the CIM was signed, and remains in force, revised, adapted and updated to suit changing needs, and it forms the basis of international freight transport law.

As European railways grew together, so Britain remained an island without a physical link to Europe and considerations of through transport were academic. In any case, the main lines had already been built to smaller loading gauges than the European standard. Yet the means to achieve such through transport were tried out on the Firth of Forth in 1850, when the first train ferry was used pending the building of a permanent link. It took the

First World War, though, to prompt the appli-cation of this technique to the English Channel. It was a logical step - rail was the only reliable, fast means of long distance transport, and much time was lost in trans-shipping from rail to ship, and ship back to rail at ports. In this case, why not ship the wagon? And that is exactly what happened, services operating from Richborough to Dunkirk and Calais, and from Southampton to Dieppe. After the war the installation at Richborough was purchased and moved to Harwich to form the British base for the first commercial ferry service in 1923. This service, to Zeebrugge in Belgium conveys freight only and continues in service to this day.

Another result of the First War, the Treaty of Versailles, gave birth to the UIC - today's focus for the development of Inter-national standards.

The Dover-Dunkirk services were not intro-duced until 1936, using locked docks at both ports to overcome the problems of high tidal ranges. This route now carries freight only, although until October 1980 it also conveyed the night ferry sleeping cars for Paris and Brussels.

The train ferry technique was the first, true roll-on/roll-off operation, but it was not until after the Second World War, though, that there came the explosive growth of roll-on/roll-off movement of lorries by several ferry opera-tors, Sealink among them. At this time, BR established a containership link between Harwich and Zeebrugge. Despite a vast increase in the movement of perishables (traditional train ferry traffic) and merchandise between Britain and Europe, the tonnage handled by the ageing train ferries dropped year by year until it seemed that this aspect of BR's freight business might be quietly laid to rest, when the ships came to the end of their useful lives.

The reason for this decline is not hard to see. BR had simply failed to compete in a changing world. When train ferries started, the only competition lay in classic break-bulk ships or the use of small containers, usually railway-owned. No worthwhile steps were taken to offer the customer a 'through' product, either in service or tariff terms. Effectively it was the sum of the national products to which the cost and delay inherent in a double trans-shipment and the sea-crossing were added. It is small wonder that this resulted in very slow transits, lack of overall co-ordination, and a positive jungle of traffic that became the specialist world of the forwarding agents.

Prior to the 1970s, nearly all of our Continental freight business was in the hands of forwarding agents; some were large multi-nationals of their time; some small family concerns with ties with specific countries or, specific commodities. Working for the agents was a 'tarifeur', the specialist among the specialists, whose knowledge of the small print of the national tariffs was his raison d'être. The tarriffs frequently bore little relation to the actual cost to the railway of carrying the goods, and the tarifeur would inevitably secure the most advantageous rate from end to end. Other services would also be looked after by the forwarding agent - customs clearance, wagon location, documentation etc.

The nature of the business was very diverse, but strictly wagonload, or less than wagonload. Imported foodstuffs dominated - perishable fruit and vegetables - and exports were mainly manu-factured goods and groupage. Hauls within Britain were short, London and South East predominating, and with the notable exception of imported fruit, transits were measured in weeks rather than days, lengthy delays at frontiers being commonplace. So it was hardly surprising that not only market share but abso-lute tonnages dropped alarmingly in the face of improvements in the competitors' products - in RO RO and container operations. By 1974, tonnage had hit an all-time low, the ageing fleet of ferries no longer offering anything like the sort of product demanded by the customer.

As we enter the 1980s, though, the situation is changing radically, and so is the market, with tonnage not only rising steadily, but having reached levels where the problems being wrestled with were those of surplus traffic rather than surplus capacity. The reasons for this marked revival have a wider significance in that they owe much to a determined attack on such problems as complex tariffs and delays at ports and relatively little to investment and new technology. Notable exceptions where investment has been of paramount importance are high capacity private wagons and TOPS, BR's computer-based wagon reporting system, which has been an indispensable tool in enabling managment to keep wagon movement under tight control and thus build customer confidence. Above all, though, there was the realisation that the train ferry product had to compete in the market place, and to be indentified, packaged and sold as a throughput transit.

The RO RO and container operator could

offer just this - a customer could load his goods, pay a single price without complex calculation, and know that the transport would be made reliably and quickly. To gain traffic, railfreight international had to do the same, and the figures show the size of the achievement.

Total train ferry tonnage (000 tonnes)

1975	605
1976	671
1977	867
1978	902
1979	1039

The completion nationwide of the TOPS system in 1975 gave a boost to all BR's freight operations, and at last gave managers the instant information they needed on which decisions could be taken to correct operating problems. Overnight customers learned that BR had nothing to hide as to the whereabouts of their wagons. Gone were the days when a customer could be told 'Your wagon left Dover two days ago, and is on its way. It will arrive sometime'. An 'open book' philosophy, and the wider use of what could have been considered purely an operating tool, has done much to restore customer confidence.

In parallel, BR seized the opportunity offered by the decision to change from vacuum to air brakes to introduce an express wagon-load service of superior quality, now marketed as 'Speedlink'. The Speedlink network, an attempt to apply trainload performance standards to selected less-than-trainload flows, was developed along carefully studied lines of route, avoiding the delays inherent in marshalling yards but providing for the rapid exchange of sections at key locations. Harwich and Dover were brought into the network at an early stage, fast overnight transits being introduced between these ports and major industrial centres.

Furthermore in 1976, a new train ferry berth was opened at Dunkerque, which was not only closer to Dover, but did not require an enclosed dock. Effectively, this cut the round trip time for ferries from 12 to 8 hours, giving a 50% boost to capacity and improved reliability. Indeed, the principal bottle-neck on this route has now become the cramped sidings at Dover, squeezed in between cliffs and foreshore, coupled with British Customs requirements. For export wagons though, adjustment of ships sailing times has provided connections from Speedlink trains via sea crossing into the fast TEEM services from Dunkerque and Zeebrugge, offering the prospect of loading a wagon in Glasgow on Day 1 and unloading it in Basle, on Day 3 - reliably.

At the same time the tariff jungle was tackled, and many of the old complex tariffs replaced by a new breed - the direct per-wagon tariff. The wagon, after all, is the unit of movement; its transport costs virtually the same whatever it is loaded with. So instead of charging a tonne - km rate for each specific commodity, the basic unit became the wagon. The new tariffs brought immediate approval from British customers, although it took time to persuade partner railways on the Continent. BR can now quote per-wagon through tariffs to France, Spain, Belgium, Holland, West Germany, Austria and Switzerland, and a new Italian tariff is in preparation.

The next and most important factor in the recovery of train ferry services was the development of a wide range of modern wagons to handle specific traffics and to suit better the customers' needs. Traditional ferry wagons were fairly straightforward, rather old-fashioned vans and flats, such as those built by BR in the 1950s. But with the increase in the transport of unfinished and finished goods, and the resultant rise in the value and volume of freight, together with modern handling techniques, wagon companies have been called on to produce vehicles to help railways compete more successfully with road and container operations. Wagon lengths have increased, many are now 20 m or more long, not only to boost capacity and thereby reduce unit costs, but also to facilitate the use of modern handling techniques and to permit larger loads to be carried. At the same time modern construction methods and the use of the lightweight materials has avioded undue increase in vehicle weight. Ease of loading is an important consideration, and many ingenious door designs have resulted to enable lift trucks to manoeuvre through them. Sliding plug-type doors give access to half the vehicle at a time, whilst vehicles in which walls and roof can be retracted have been developed. Many wagons are built to handle specific traffics such as motor car parts and effectively form part of the production line. Load stowing and retaining devices are increasingly fitted to reduce damage in transit and speed up loading. With the need to reduce transit times, so as to offer a more attractive service, achieve greater productivity and ensure that freight trains do not obstruct high speed passenger trains, wagons running at 100 or 120 km/h are now the standard. The increase in speed has been made possible by improving suspension designs, the adoption of better braking systems and the move to longer wheelbase wagons.

Specialised wagons have been developed in recent years for ferry services, starting with a sliding roof design built by SBA (Société des Ferryboats Belgo-Anglaise). These four-wheeled wagons were among the first of the new breed of easy access wagons and are in extensive use.

The major impetus in the wagon development field has come, however, from private wagon builders; private wagon ownership has, of course, long been accepted and encouraged, and the arrival of the 80 tonnes gross four-axle covered wagons of the VTG and Cargowaggon companies produces a customer reaction of unparalleled rapidity and positiveness. Of similar characteristics they are 21.7m long, and are fitted with two sliding doors per side which give a clear width of 10m when open, with a vertical clearance of 2.4m. Large lift trucks can be used for loading as the floor can take wheel loads of up to 5 tonnes. Securing eyes

fixed to the underframe, sidewalls and roof enable the goods to be lashed down.

VTG have also introduced some versatile coil carrying wagons for steel traffic. Built by Linke-Hofmann-Busch, they have a capacity of 60.5 tonnes. Three telescopic hoods provide simple access for loading and automatically lock when closed. Adjustable fixings secure the coils. The words 'single-handed' are perhaps overworked, but it is impressive to see and experience the opening or closing of the telescopic hood performed 'single-handed'.

For specialised bulk dry traffics, the Polybulk system has found favour - particularly for grain and china clay; the goods are contained in a polythene inner lining (hence the name) which can be quickly changed to facilitate return loading.

Traffic from Spain and Portugal presents special problems because of the change of gauge, and the Transfesa campany has developed a specialised wagon which has axles changed at the French/Spanish frontier. Fitted with ventilated sides they are used for perishables traffic and it is a sign of Transfesa's faith in train ferry that they have now developed a major railhead at Paddock Wood in Kent. The time taken for the axle change is minimal, with four wagons a time being processed in an average of 5 minutes.

For temperature-controlled traffics, a substantial fleet of refrigerated wagons was built by the railways subsidiary Interfrigo, and these still form a substantial segment of our traffic.

As traffic increased in the late seventies as these various factors came to bear, the train ferry product picked up, as has been shown by the tonnages carried, and far from dying slowly new life was breathed in, and expansion and reinvestment were evidently possible and justifiable.

With capacity at Dover under severe constraint because of the port layout and the size of the 1936 ferry dock, BR had to look to its route based on Harwich to provide the substantial increase in ship capacity that was, by 1979, clearly necessary. Accordingly a strategy was developed which resulted in the 3 year charter in August 1980 of the Speedlink Vanguard; with a capacity of 56 standard wagons, compared with 22 on the previously existing ships, daily throughput was raised by 50% and eased capacity problems on the route to Zeebrugge, at the same time enabling the Harwich-Dunkerque service to be increased to a daily frequency. This charter is in support of the much bigger project to construct two really large 'Jumbo' ferries for the Zeebrugge route, each capable of transporting 104 wagons. The first of these ships is due to be introduced in 1983 and will further dramatically increase capacity on the route. They will offer the opportunity to develop train load traffic in our international services for the first time, and it is not difficult to envisage the economical and attractive nature of such a train load movement, from, say, a private siding in the Ruhr to a private siding in the West Midlands, within 48 hours! Yet with

Jumbo that will be a practical proposition and we are working hard to translate it into reality.

As traffic expands, and the problem of shipping space is dealt with, so the capacity of port procedures comes under strain. BR is working closely with HM Customs to improve matters in the short term, and has introduced a system of remote facsimile reproduction to transmit documents ahead of incoming wagons. Further, BR and HM Customs revised their documents presentation methods, with the result that import documentation can be presented ahead of wagons arrival and cleared as the wagons come ashore. Prior to this system, only 15% of imported wagons cleared Harwich within 24 hours. Now, over 70% achieve this regularly - most of them in under 12 hours.

The Jumbo project is seen as supportive of - not competitive with - the ultimate goal, the construction of a Channel Tunnel. There will almost certainly be a continuing demand for one train ferry route to carry dangerous goods. These already use Harwich-Zeebrugge, and the Jumbo ships will greatly increase our capacity to handle them. It is probable that dangerous goods will be excluded from a Tunnel on safety grounds, and yet the market is a greatly expanding one. In any case, there should be little difficulty in finding buyers for the ships should they be made redundant.

There is no cause either for resting on the laurels of past achievements. Whilst TOPS provides wagon control within the UK, ideally this must be extended into Europe, and direct links with the SNCF GCTM system are being studied. For the future, the developing UIC-sponsored HERMES data interchange system will enable tight control and complete information on wagon movements. There is always room for improving the quality of the product, and the first steps have been taken to develop on an international scale the joint marketing and investment policies which are essential to ensure a coherent approach to common problems.

We conclude, therefore, that the prospect before us is one of growth and expansion of the international railfreight business, particularly in bulk, a sector which we forsee making a valuable and increasing contribution to over-all railfreight performance. The balance of costs is moving in favour of long hauls by rail, and with the economies of scale we will achieve with our Jumbo ships, we believe we have a product which has a great future. Certainly there is a great deal of work to be done, but the rewards are rich and we are confident of achieving them.

C38/81

Standardisation — its effect on freight economics

D R TAYLOR, CEng, MIMechE
British Railways Board Headquarters, Derby

SYNOPSIS   The potential benefits of standardisation of rolling stock have long been recognised, and methods for achieving this are suggested.   Reference is made to the progress towards standardisation made by our predecessors, and particularly the work of the Railway Clearing House.   The relationship of standardisation to cost is examined as it affects different stages of a wagon's life and use. The cost of three current or recent builds of wagon are broken down on a percentage basis into six significant areas.   Reference is made to BR's work towards standardisation and the need for discipline to achieve standardisation.   Finally, relating to the theme of the Symposium, comment is made that railways are, in relation to work effort, inherently low energy consumers.

INTRODUCTION

The potential benefits of the standardisation of railway rolling stock have long been recognised.   As this Symposium deals particularly with freight rolling stock it is of interest to recall a paper presented to the Institution of Locomotive Engineers, in February 1919, entitled 'Suggestions for Standardised Wagon Designs for British Railways'.(1)

This paper was read, at the Leeds Centre of the Institution, the presiding Chairman being Mr, later Sir, H.N. Gresley - indeed a famous name in railway engineering annals.   The Paper was written against the backcloth of the Great War 1914-1918 and prior to the creation of the four main line railway companies, by the amalgamations of 1923.   Because the overall transport scenario was, at that time, very different, I do not intend to spend much time in referring to the points made in the Paper but nevertheless, it is of interest to state that the Author proposed five standard types of wagon:

```
12 ton Open Wagon - with high sides
12  "     "      "   -  "  medium sides
                              (to fall)
12  "     "      "   -  "  low sides
12  "  Covered Wagon
20  "  Open Wagon for coal
```

It was acknowledged also that there may be an on-going necessity for individual designs for special work and for service purposes.   Indeed at the time, it appears that there were about

1 500 000 wagons in existence, half of which were privately owned.   Presently the corresponding totals, revenue only, are 155 000 wagons of which approximately 18 500 are privately owned.

It is interesting to note that, at Nationalisation in 1948 , there were 1 200 000 wagons and as recently as 1958 the total was still in excess of 1 000 000.   By 1966 the number had reduced to 550 000 and by 1976 the fleet totalled just below 200 000.   Current plans envisage a further drastic reduction in BR wagons over the next 5 years to a projected total of approximately 54 000 revenue earning wagons.   Does this comparison suggest that the present day problems of standardisation should be more readily resolved?   Perhaps more germane to to-day's Symposium was the realisation, expressed more than once, in the Paper, of the benefits that standardisation confers upon the maintenance activity, and I quote,

> 'From a practical point of view it is chiefly the question of maintenance which causes those responsible for wagon upkeep to consider standardisation. Owing to its absence a much greater number of spare parts is required for wagon repairs, entailing much expense and delay in effecting the release of damaged vehicles.'

As delegates to this Symposium, with diverse interests in Railway matters, there is one common factor which unites us all and this is the ambition to achieve a profitable Railway.   To this end, it is important that all techniques are reviewed constantly; standardisation is one such technique.

---

(1)   BAZIN J.R. (M) 'Suggestions for Standardised Wagon Designs for British Railways', Institution of Locomotive Engineers. Presented Doncaster 25 February 1919, Paper No.71.

STANDARDISATION

Standardisation is a much misused word and suffers from the fact that it tends to mean 'all things to all men'. In order that there is no dubiety on what is meant by standardisation the following definition is given.

To progress by rationalisation, reduction of types, to the minimum range of vehicle types embodying the maximum number of common components, which will carry out the specified business.

This definition suggests that activity towards standardisation must be directed in two ways:

i) For new vehicles - a critical examination of all new designs to restrict, as far as practicable, compatible with the specification, the design changes to ensure that no new designs are introduced where an existing design will meet the requirements of the specification and that component parts are selected from a standardised range.

ii) For existing vehicles - an energetic and detailed examination of the components and materials with a view to rationalising the number of different varieties used.

It is recognised that such a course of action particularly as that advocated for new designs will bring forth the charge that innovation and progress is being stultified. This may be partially true but it is a discipline that must be followed if any significant progress is to be made towards standardisation and through this to a reduction in costs. In any event, I believe a good measure of ingenuity is often required to enable a standardised design or component to be used.

It should be recognised that our predecessors, in the years following the 1923 amalgamations, did achieve a high level of component standardisation through the efforts of the Railway Clearing House. All basic components were standardised and designs issued with RCH drawing numbers. To this day, to a limited extent, these drawings are still in use by all parts of the Industry.

I believe it is apposite to quote an extract from a paper (2) presented to the Institution of Locomotive Engineers in 1950 by C.A. Gammon, Chairman of the Wagon Standards Committee, which referred to the setting up of the Carriage & Wagon Superintendents' (later CMEs) Committee in 1885 under the aegis of the Railway Clearing House,

---

(2) GAMMON C.A. - Standardisation and Design of Goods and Mineral Wagons as Applied to British Railways, Institution of Locomotive Engineers Paper No.496 1950.

'when an urgent need arose to formulate Standards for the ever increasing number of privately owned coal and other types of wagons required to meet the expanding industrialism...".

The first 'standard' drawings and specifications laying down general dimensions for the body and certain components of coal wagons, became operative in 1887.

You will realise that to-day we are not breaking new ground.

FINANCIAL TRENDS

No one, at this Symposium, needs to be reminded that costs have risen over the past few years and show every indication of continuing to do so, certainly in the short term. Associated with this situation are high interest rates which mean that investment in rolling stock can only be achieved at a premium cost. The situation may well arise and indeed may already have arisen where the manufacturing costs of rolling stock are so high that the investment, allowing for a reasonable profit margin, cannot be met from the revenue accruing to the Business. To try to solve the problem by raising freight charges will mean that the railway, as a mode of transport, will be less attractive, with the result that the traffic which is on offer will gravitate towards the road.

From a commercial, if not from a survival point of view it is essential that the engineer seeks technical solutions which will bring about cheaper manufacturing costs and lower maintenance costs. Furthermore, not only must the engineer 'look to his laurels' but equally the operator and the user must ensure that the high cost rolling stock is used, to its maximum capacity.

EXAMINATION OF COSTS

In order to examine how standardisation may contribute to a reduction in costs it is at first necessary to appreciate where the costs arise. This is perhaps best done by considering the significant stages of a wagon's life.

DESIGN

Traditionally the Business establishes the need for a type of wagon to convey a particular commodity. From this requirement a technical specification is evolved and from this, the specific design. It follows that the resulting vehicle is very suited to its purpose but there has only to be a change in the purpose to render that particular type of wagon redundant. Fortunately, it is often possible to use the wagon for some other purpose but bearing in mind that the life span of a wagon is of the order of 25 to 35 years the risk of diminished requirement is always present, and hence the ability to modify the design becomes attractive. To this end, it is worth examining the practicability of designing a number of standard components in such a way that a wagon can be 'tailor made' to suit the specific purposes of the Business. It is not suggested that in pure design time this method will make a large contribution to a reduction in cost but it will provide the ability to supply the Business with a wagon which meets their requirements in a predictable manner, at the lowest cost and furthermore, the possibility of modification, if the traffic pattern changes.

The principles outlined are being examined by BR in relation to the underframe (see Fig. 1).

MANUFACTURING

The traditional method of manufacture is to jig assemble the main components, i.e. underframes, bodies, doors etc and bring these together to construct the complete wagon. Because the Business requires wagons of different configurations, it means that the jigs and fixtures from one build of wagon are not suitable for the next and hence there are additional costs in the rejigging process. It is a matter of fact that the majority of builds in the private sector are of small batch numbers and the cost of jigging must add disproportionately to the cost of the wagon. If the concept of standard components be adopted it would mean that standard jigs could be used in their construction and indeed, it would be possible to pre-manufacture such components, in volume, minimising the manufacturing costs.

TESTING

Each new design of wagon has to be submitted for riding, and braking tests to satisfy the Railway that it is safe to operate, on their system and more often than not some remedial action is required to the design, in order to enable it to attain the various defined parameters. This imposes additional delays and adds to the costs, before the wagon is released to traffic. This delay amounts to a loss of revenue which can be ill-afforded by any sector of the railway business.

I am not suggesting that standardisation will eliminate the need for testing, but that standardisation of components, for example suspensions, could materially help to reduce the delay to the wagon entering service and earning revenue.

MAINTENANCE

The advantages of standardisation of components on wagons is probably greater in the area of maintenance than in any other aspect and, in order to draw out these advantages, it is helpful to sub-divide the general heading of maintenance into a number of sub-headings.

a) Provision of Spares

When an industry has invested scarce resources in a wagon, then it is important that its availability for revenue earning traffic is maximised. One factor which often prevents the user from securing the maximum availability arises when a wagon is stopped awaiting spares. If there is a multitude of types of wagons, each with differing detail components, then the

acquisition of spares and even the identification of the required components is time consuming. During this lost time the wagon is not earning its keep. In this respect I am not thinking only of the more important components of a wagon, but also the minor details such as steps, stanchions, axleguards, etc which although of a minor nature, can determine whether a vehicle is fit for service or not.

Vehicles constructed to full RIV standards for International Traffic do, of course, have to comply with standard Regulations concerning the interchangeability of parts. This does not always mean that items are produced to the same drawings but complete interchangeability must be achieved and components branded accordingly. BR engineers are taking part in an increasing amount of UIC/ORE work and this is reflected in the decisions already taken and itemised later in the paper.

b) Artisan Knowledge

In the past, traditional wagon maintenance practices have relied upon the craft knowledge of the artisan, but I think that, in the future, we may be forced, as an industry, to employ staff of a calibre who may not have the traditional skills of a carriage & wagon man and thus the engineer must arrive at a solution whereby the onus on the artisan is reduced to a minimum. Standardisation of components will go a long way to meeting these anticipated difficulties and optimising availability.

c) Predictable Costs

It is often a complaint of wagon owners that maintenance costs of wagons vary from type to type and it is frequently difficult to determine if the price being charged is correct, because of the variations of the particular wagon design.

If an approach based on the use of standard components could be adopted then, by basic method study techniques, it should be possible to predict accurately the work content within maintenance and repairs. This would give a better estimate of the total cost of wagon maintenance and repairs, leading to more accurate budget predictions and greater confidence on the predicted earnings of a wagon.

d) Reliability

The other critical factor in obtaining the maximum utilisation of any wagon is a high degree of reliability.. It is accepted, generally speaking, that the level of reliability is already high, but from time to time wagons are introduced which contain features in their design, which affect reliability. With the standardisation approach, one could anticipate that only the best, proved practices would be designed into the standards and thus it should be possible to achieve a better overall level of reliability.

SCOPE FOR STANDARDISATION

It is not the intention in this paper to set down every component which could be rationalised or standardised, but to give some guidance based on the work being undertaken by BR which illustrates the concept of standardisation. In this connection, I draw your attention to Fig 2. These diagrams represent, as percentages, the breakdown of the total wagon cost related to six significant areas of the wagon, for example the body, including floors, doors etc, the underframe including couplings and Drawgear and so on. The three wagon types shown are current or recent builds:

1) 2 axle 46t GLW Wagon for carrying steel (SPA) air braked with disc brakes on all wheels and maximum speed of 75 mph (40t GLW)

2) 2 axle 46t GLW Hopper Wagon for carrying power station coal (HAA). Fitted with doorgear operated by lineside equipment or manually.

3) 102t Bogie Steel Wagon for carrying various steel products (BBA). Air braked with discbrakes on all wheels and maximum speed of 75 mph (80t GLW).

Obviously, these are three very different types of wagon and I do not want to suggest that too much should be read into the percentage figures quoted - a lot more work on these is necessary before this can be done - but, I think that the figures do point to areas where some detailed investigation is necessary, e.g. the area of suspensions, wheelsets, axleboxes and Bearings and underframe brakework. Accordingly, I propose to comment on these and others.

SUSPENSION

Experience on BR track has shown that the UIC Double Link suspension does not perform well particularly at speeds over 60 mph. BR are adhering to the decision taken some years ago that, wherever possible, the BR Single Link suspension will be used. This is an area where development is a continuing process and for heavy axleloads e.g. 25.5t and some special wagons changes are necessary. The standard links are still used but incorporate traction rods for longitudinal control of wheelsets.

WHEELSETS

One can well realise that over the last 150 years, the industry has arrived at a situation where a multitude of different wheelsets are employed. During the past 2 or 3 years a great effort has been made to rationalise types and eliminate redundant designs. A major problem in tackling the latter issue is the longevity of BR vehicles. Even when a wagon leaves revenue earning service it may then enter a further phase of life, as a service vehicle, with a total life of some 50 years. Provision of spares for these wagons is a continual, and continuing, problem. Rationalising of wheelsets for new designs was easier and was essentially linked to the decision, at that time, to standardise on cartridge bearing units of 4 basic sizes of 120, 130, 140 and 150mm diameter. Sizes of wheels

are of course the subject of limits imposed by the Civil Engineer and are related to the speed of the vehicle (see Fig 3).

Further rationalisation has been influenced by the decision of the UIC to up-rate their standard 130 d axle from 20t to 22t by revising the design of the journal. BR have therefore decided to standardise on 2 basic axle sizes for future freight designs

130mm journal; 2m. journal centres for axleloads up to 22t
150mm journal; 2.07m. journal centres for axleloads up to 25.5t

The larger journal centres of 2.07m for the 150mm axle has been retained to enable disc brakes to be more readily fitted to the wheels. It has already been established that wheel mounted disc brakes can be fitted to 2m journal centres for the lower axle load.

In arriving at this decision consideration was given in the interests of standardisation to the possible use of the largest journal diameter, on the assumption that it would more than adequately serve the lower axleloads albeit accepting the penalty of additional cost and weight. The possibility was finally discarded because of the difficulties arising at the wheel-seat due to the various diameters and the consequential need to vary the axle design geometry.

AXLEBOXES

BR have standardised on the use of cartridge bearing units and these will now be of the 2 sizes 130mm and 150mm dia. The 130mm unit is a new item to suit the up-rated UIC axle with its revised journal.

SPRINGS

BR have taken the initiative in the use of friction controlled parabolic springs, as replacements for the conventional laminated springs. All new 2 axle wagons with the exception of High Capacity Coal Wagons (HAA) are fitted with these springs and existing wagons are being re-equipped, when the occasion demands. A greatly increased life, equating to the life of the wagon is expected of the springs, at no additional cost. Through its participation in the ORE B12, Standardisation of Wagons Committee the views and experience of BR are being ventilated and it is anticipated that such springs will shortly become a UIC standard fitting.

BUFFERS & DRAWGEAR

For many years BR have used hydraulic buffers exclusively on new wagons and this practice has been extended in some cases to existing vehicles where replacement of old types has proved difficult. Attempts have been made over the past 2 years to rationalise the types in use and BR have now decided to standardise on just 2 types, for new vehicles. These will be a round headed type for 2 axle wagons and a rectangular headed buffer for bogie wagons. Both types will be of 620mm projection in line with international practice to align with the use of international screw couplings. This coupling and buffer projection will be used on all new wagons except where the Operating Department dictate the use of instantor couplings, for marshalling purposes, e.g. HAA wagons. BR have recognised that the latest UIC/ORE developments in drawgear have resulted in an arrangement that is superior to the present BR type. This latest swivel type drawhook with rubber springs of higher capacity will be used on all new BR wagons. The private owners have been advised of this, in the usual manner via the Joint Technical Committee. British Rail are represented on both UIC and ORE Committees dealing with buffing and drawgear and a close watch is being kept on all developments.

BRAKEGEAR

As all connected with the industry are aware, BR decided on the 2 pipe air system several years ago and this policy is being maintained. It has been decided that all service vehicles will be fitted with tread brakes using composition blocks to obtain information on the practical performance of these blocks and reduce the amount of maintenance on these wagons. For revenue earning stock BR intend to pursue the present policy of using disc brakes unless there are overriding technical or cost considerations. In such cases tread brakes with CI or composition blocks will be used.

Attempts are being made to bring about the standardisation of all air brake components so as to achieve interchangeability. Difficulties have been met with items such as distributors but it is intended to pursue this course vigorously, as it is felt that use of common fittings will greatly facilitate both manufacture and maintenance.

UNDERFRAMES

The use of standard underframes for different types of wagons is not new. The old RCH series included several designs of underframe for various wagon types and their use was widespread. To reduce the cost of producing new jigs and fixtures BR have decided to investigate the use of a structure, for 2 axle wagons, incorporating common sections which can be varied in length to suit the various requirements. It is accepted that there may be a weight penalty for shorter wagons but this should be outweighed by lower first costs and subsequent maintenance. The underframe end structure will be retained as common for all wagons and it is interesting to note that a similar approach has been adopted for bogie wagons by the ORE B12 Committee.

Again it has to be accepted that some wagons will fall outside this arrangement e.g. Freightliners with low deck height and small wheels, but wherever possible standard components will be specified.

As might have been expected, the foregoing itemised comments refer principally to the situation as it affects new designs of wagons and justifiably one might ask what is going to be done in respect of existing wagons. Quite evidently the expenditure involved to effect changes to standard components, unless this can

be done on the basis of replacement for life expired components, can never be justified, particularly in these days of severe financial restraint, but it is believed that considerable scope exists for greater rationalisation of components and the ways and means of devoting greater resources to this activity are being explored, although a considerable amount of work has been done already on such components as suspension eyebolts, drawhooks, drawbars and laminated springs.

ADMINISTRATION

Standardisation will not happen of its own accord and to achieve any significant progress will demand a discipline that not only ensures that standards are adhered to, but also questions diligently the need for departure from agreed standards. Instinctively, it is more attractive to the designer to be able to pursue his art, with no, or few, constraints and furthermore let it be acknowledged that it is often tedious, if not difficult, to check back on what has gone before. This is an area, data retrieval, where the computer can bring considerable benefits and BR have developed a system, Parts Data Base, which will be extremely useful but which alas, at the present time, is hostage to the severe financial position.

The onus of adhering to Standards does not rest only with the designer but also with the Business who in developing the Business Specification for a wagon must do so conscious of the benefits of standardisation. It is nevertheless the duty of the designer to be able to highlight the disadvantages (in cost) of not doing so.

On the subject of the Business Specification, although not connected directly with standardisation, I believe there is an ever present need to challenge constructively the stipulated requirements to be sure that these are strictly necessary to achieve the purpose of the wagon and not just desirable extras which can considerably affect the cost of the wagon and the overall economics of the project. I am aware that in some cases these requirements are determined by BR and are necessary to conform to a stated policy but nevertheless, the principle I am at pains to emphasize is the need to challenge the requirements to be satisfied that they are as stated and are essential.

GENERAL

Bearing in mind the theme of this Symposium, 'Rail Freight, a Contribution to the Conservation of Energy' it is worth reminding everyone that the railways are inherently a low energy consumer in relation to work effort. This matter is currently a subject of study by the Transport Commission of the European Parliament. Conservatively, based on information supplied by the UK Advisory Council on Energy Conservation, the energy consumption of rail and road is of the order of 1.0: 2.5, in favour of rail. On this theme it is relevant to refer to Mr K. Taylor's Railway Division Chairman's Address, in 1979, where the following Table was produced. Your particular attention is drawn to the section dealing with freight (see Table 1).

More specifically, the following information in respect of a Cl 56, 3250 hp locomotive hauling a 1000 tonne trailing load, over the East coast main line is interesting (see Table 2).

The implications of handling a similar load by road are evident, and should, I believe, make everyone that much more determined to capitalise, on the advantages, and with this objective make standardisation work.

CONCLUSION

I am not a believer in standardisation for standardisation's sake but I believe that by following a sensible well thought out and defined policy of standardisation economies can be made and a better product produced. None of these benefits will accrue without a concerted and determined effort on everyones' part. British Rail is committed.

ACKNOWLEDGMENTS

The Author acknowledges his indebtedness to the Chief Mechanical & Electrical Engineer, British Railways Board, for permission to publish this Paper and the help that he has received from his colleagues.

Table 1   General energy consumption comparisons

Passenger ∕	Average load factor %	Average MJ/pass km
Inter-City electric train	45	1.0
Inter-City diesel train	45	0.9
Express coach	65	0.4
Scheduled aircraft	65	3.9
Car on motorway	2 passengers	1.6
Car rural	1.7 passengers	2.0
Commuter train	25	1.1
Underground train	14	1.6
Double-decker bus	25	0.8
Car	1.5 passengers	3.1

Freight ≠		Range MJ/tonne km
Rail:	bulk freight	0.4-1.2
	general merchandise	0.5-1.7
Road:	bulk materials	1.4-2.4
	general merchandise	0.9-3.5

These figures give a general view but do not form a reliable basis for assessing potential energy savings from modal transfers for particular groups of traffic. Such changes are often contemplated because the rates of consumption in the alternatives differ significantly from the general figures.

∕   Energy Paper No 10 BR facts and figures

≠   Energy Paper No 24 BR facts and figures

Table 2   Class 56 Locomotive — 1000 tonne trailing load

London - Newcastle (265.8 miles)

Class 56	45 mile/h	60 mile/h	75 mile/h
Overall time	359 mins	283 mins	253 mins
Average speed	44.4 mile/h	56.3 mile/h	63.0 mile/h
Ratio average/maximum speed	98.7%	93.8%	84%
Fuel consumption	380 gal.	515 gal	580 gal.

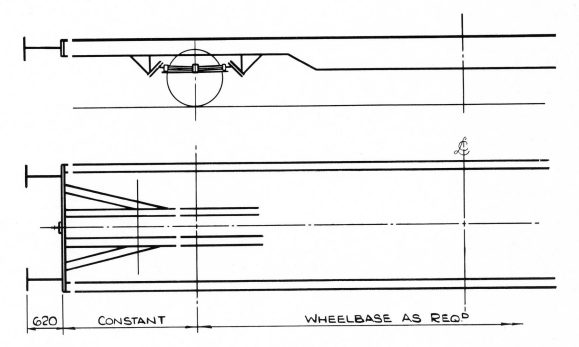

Fig 1   Underframe: standard components

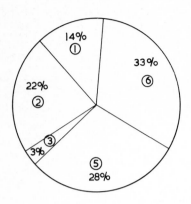

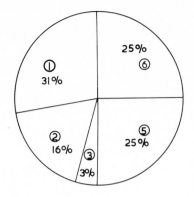

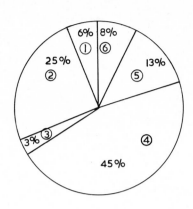

SPA.
2 AXLE WAGON

HAA.
2 AXLE WAGON

BBA.
BOGIE STEEL

KEY.
① — BODY, INCLUDING FLOORS, DOORS ETC.
② — UNDERFRAME INCLUDING COUPLINGS AND DRAWGEAR.
③ — BUFFERS.
④ — BOGIES, INCLUDING BOGIE BRAKEWORK.
⑤ — SUSPENSIONS, WHEELSETS, AXLEBOXES AND BEARINGS.
⑥ — UNDERFRAME BRAKEWORK.

Fig 2   Breakdown of wagon costs

2 - AXLE WAGONS.

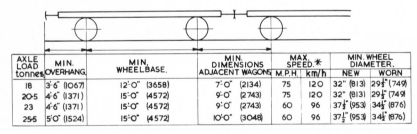

AXLE LOAD tonnes	MIN. OVERHANG.	MIN. WHEELBASE.	MIN. DIMENSIONS ADJACENT WAGONS	MAX. SPEED.* M.P.H.	km/h	MIN. WHEEL DIAMETER. NEW	WORN
18	3'-6" (1067)	12'-0" (3658)	7'-0" (2134)	75	120	32" (813)	29½" (749)
20.5	4'-6" (1371)	15'-0" (4572)	9'-0" (2743)	75	120	32" (813)	29½" (749)
23	4'-6" (1371)	15'-0" (4572)	9'-0" (2743)	60	96	37½" (953)	34½" (876)
25.5	5'-0" (1524)	15'-0" (4572)	10'-0" (3048)	60	96	37½" (953)	34½" (876)

* MAX SPEED OF 75 M.P.H.(120 km/h) IS ONLY PERMITTED SUBJECT TO SUSPENSION PERFORMANCE BEING ACCEPTABLE TO C.M. & E.E.(B.R-B) THE RIGHT IS RESERVED TO IMPOSE ANY LOWER MAX. SPEEDS.

FOR AXLELOADS ABOVE 20.5 tonnes, BOGIES MUST BE OF PRIMARY SUSPENSION TYPE.

FOR AXLELOADS OF 20.5 tonnes OR BELOW, BOGIES OF PRIMARY SUSPENSION TYPE ARE RECOMMENDED.

BOGIE WAGONS.

AXLE LOAD tonnes	MIN. OVERHANG	MIN. WHEELBASE	MIN. DISTANCE BETWEEN INNER WHEELS.	MIN. WHEELBASE	MIN. DIMENSIONS ADJACENT WAGONS.	MAX. SPEED.* M.P.H.	km/h	MIN. WHEEL DIAMETER. NEW	WORN
14	4'-6"(1371)	5'-11"(1800)	16'-0" (4877)	5'-11" (1800)	9'-0" (2743)	75	120	28½" (724)	27" (686)
16.5	4'-6"(1371)	5'-11"(1800)	18'-0" (5486)	5'-11" (1800)	9'-0" (2743)	75	120	28½" (724)	27" (686)
18	4'-6"(1371)	5'-11"(1800)	20'-0" (6096)	5'-11" (1800)	9'-0" (2743)	75	120	32" (813)	29½" (749)
20.5	4'-6"(1371)	5'-11"(1800)	25'-0" (7620)	5'-11" (1800)	9'-0" (2743)	75	120	32" (813)	29½" (749)
22	4'-6"(1371)	5'-11"(1800)	25'-0" (7620)	5'-11" (1800)	9'-0" (2743)	60	96	36" (914)	33" (838)
23	4'-9"(1448)	6'-6¾"(2000)	27'-6" (8382)	6'-6¾"(2000)	9'-6" (2896)	60	96	37½" (953)	34½" (876)
25.5	5'-0"(1524)	6'-6¾"(2000)	30'-0" (9144)	6'-6¾"(2000)	10'-0" (3048)	60	96	37½" (953)	34½" (876)

NOTE.   THE ABOVE DIMENSIONS ARE REQUIRED FOR FUTURE BUILDS OF WAGONS TO MAINTAIN OPTIMUM ROUTE AVAILABILITY FOR VEHICLES HAVING THE AXLE WEIGHTS SPECIFIED.

C.C.E. MAY ACCEPT WAGONS WITH LOWER DIMENSIONS THAN ABOVE, BUT ONLY ON ROUTES TO BE CLEARLY SPECIFIED AND ACCEPTED BEFORE BUILDING.

N.B. EXISTING WAGONS CONTINUE UNDER PRESENT CONDITIONS.

Fig 3   Minimum dimensions relative to axle spacing
and loads on freight vehicles

C34/81

A new look at brakework

D W TANDY, TEng (CEI), MITEME
The Standard Railway Wagon Company Limited

SYNOPSIS   Until 1970 the tread brake, with cast iron blocks, was the primary braking medium for freight vehicles in the U.K. During the following five years, the disc brake took a firm hold of the market offering a reduced tare weight and ·space-saving opportunities which were a great advantage in such wagons as two axle hoppers.

This paper studies the route taken by The Standard Railway Wagon Company in developing alternative braking systems using high friction, composition brake blocks and a simplified actuation system, maintaining the tare weight and space-saving advantages required in modern wagons.

INTRODUCTION

Until the late 1960s/early 1970s little consideration was given to the tare weight of wagons. In fact, some of the load to tare ratios of wagons before this period are very poor. But since then, more and more emphasis has been placed on reducing the tare weight and maximising payload.

One area which has produced a substantial reduction in weight is in the brakework. For many years wagon brakework had included a complicated array of levers, slack adjusters, cylinders, pull rods, brake shafts and their supporting bracketry weighing well over a tonne and a half.

Hopper wagons had to have complicated brake arrangements situated on top of the wagon frame which was heavy, looked ugly and restricted hopper and doorgear design. The biggest impact upon the industry in this respect was the introduction of the disc brake fitted one disc per axle. Overnight it reduced the tare weight of wagons by about one tonne, which meant one tonne of extra payload every trip for a little capital expenditure. The maintenance was expected to be lower as fewer parts were involved and disc pads were expected to last substantially longer than cast iron brake blocks.

There was a further advantage with the use of disc brakes and that was the space it offered between the wheels. This was used to great advantage in hopper wagons with bottom doors being extended in some cases the length of the wagon between the axles. The disc brake was a very neat, compact system braking each axle independently and required only an air pipe connecting between opposite ends of the wagon. Its one drawback at this stage was that it needed a screw parking brake because the hand effort required a mechanical advantage to the cylinder greater than the conventional hand lever

could provide. In fact it would have needed a hand lever with something like a 1.5 metre stroke to apply the brake with enough effort to hold a loaded wagon on the required 1 in 40 slope with an effort of 490N.

The screw brake could supply this mechanical advantage but it required an indicator to show when the parking brake was on. When this indicator failed parking brakes were left on and owing to the efficiency of the disc brake, this often resulted in wheel flats and an expensive repair. Despite this, the advantages gained enabled the disc brake to rule the design of wagon brakes throughout most of the 1970s. Many good wagons were built because of the freedom which they offered and operators gained the advantage of lower tare weight and therefore increased payload.

THE NEED FOR A NEW APPROACH

With the discovery of oil off the Scottish coast, more utilisation of the highland routes became essential, particularly between Perth and Inverness. With the introduction of the heavy freight wagons in this traffic, it soon became apparent that the disc brake fitted to one wheel per axle was not sufficient and that for this route in particular, all wheels would require to be braked. This subsequently has become the norm and now all disc braked wagons, unless on restricted low risk routes, are fitted with a disc brake on all wheels.

The double disc application is a very good brake, reducing the heat input into the wheel substantially, which was the main cause for the single disc problems, thereby increasing predicted wheel life, cheek disc life and disc pad life. However, this change resulted in an increase in the tare weight, defeating some of the advantages previously gained and more particularly an increase in cost. During this period, wagon prices in general were spiralling and the substantial price increase, to already expensive brake equipment, was more than the market could tolerate and other options had to be investigated.

THE NEW DESIGN

After some months of investigations and many partial designs we finally decided to return to a tread brake but operated with a much simplified operating linkage. This system required the use of non-ferrous blocks which offer a coefficient of friction of approximately 0.3. We initially chose the TBL 803 block which is made mainly from fibre glass and does not contain asbestos.

Using this high friction we calculated back from the required stopping distance (Figure 1) to find the load in each lever of the conventional rigging. We found that the effort required in the pull rod operating the wheel leverage was similar to that produced by the S.A.B. disc brake combined cylinder and slack adjuster unit.

This very much simplified the traditional clasp brake arrangement enabling us to eliminate much of the heavy rigging normally situated in the centre of the wagon. It also divorced the brakes on each axle and looked neat enough to compete with the disc brake (Figure 4).

TESTING AND SERVICE MONITORING

From the initial design we produced a prototype and a test rig which we used to confirm the designed block loads and piston strokes. For service evaluation we borrowed and converted a hopper wagon which was originally fitted with one wheel disc brake. As our new design operates at the same air pressures and volumes, there was no need to modify the air controlling equipment. Once modified, we carried out further load cell tests and then put the wagon into service. It was first intended to run the wagon over Shap and Beattock but this was not possible, therefore the wagon was operated between Skipton and Middlesbrough. This prototype set was a little heavier than the original disc arrangement but it would save about 800 kg over the cast iron brake rigging and about 500 kg over the double disc system. A further advantage was that the parking brake was operated by a lever.

Further testing included the building of 20 x 46 tonne Class "A" tank wagons, one of which was slip tested confirming the calculated stopping distances (Figure 2), and 28 x 51 tonne tank wagons for carrying Caustic Soda. This was in 1977 and in subsequent years to 1980, 150 units were built for use in various services. These wagons were and still are, in services which include single wagons working in cast iron blocked trains and disc braked trains and some in block trains, all fitted with this system. Some of the routes covered fairly flat country and others steep gradients, including the Peak Forest run from Buxton to Manchester. To this point, progress had been deliberately slow until we were quite sure that the blocks in particular would operate satisfactorily. As wagons entered service we paid them regular visits to examine the blocks and rigging, one set of wagons operating the Manchester area and adjacent to our Heywood works was ideal for this purpose. We periodically removed the blocks for examination of metal pick-up and to check the condition of the wheels. After three years of successful operation, we then had enough confidence to try wagons between Perth and Inverness. British Railways organised the tests for April 1980 and they were designed to find the operating limit of the system. Sixteen runs were made, operating at various braking powers to as little as 23% of the total train weight, and the brakes held up well.

During this period we learned a number of lessons in the use of non-ferrous blocks. We found that most of the metal pick-up occurred in wet weather, especially with new blocks and newly machined wheels. By profiling the block to the wheel to reduce the bedding in period, the pick-up was substantially reduced. A change to the TBL 804 block was a further improvement which virtually eliminates pick-up as we knew it. These same changes have also reduced wheel damage caused by dragging brakes. In general we have found that this wheel damage is less than that caused by other braking systems, such as wheel flats with disc brakes. It usually involves scoring of the tread which in most cases does not need machining but is left to roll out over the next few loaded journeys. By far the biggest problem found is that of taper wear to the blocks which causes premature scrapping of blocks with still a lot of material unused. Initially we thought that this was mainly caused by using blocks which weigh one quarter of that for which the back was designed. By studying the design in more detail, we now know that the angle at which the main loads are applied is a major factor (Figure 3) and with a simple re-design, more efficient use of the blocks is possible.

FUTURE DEVELOPMENT

With four successful years behind us we are now in the process of using this experience to re-design the system to produce an even lighter, simpler system which utilises the blocks more efficiently. A prototype set is currently under rig testing which is intended to evaluate the effect of wheel and block wear on the efficiency of the system. The new layout is expected to reduce the tare weight by a further half tonne, having fewer levers and pins and even less maintenance will be required. It is also designed to be bench assembled for offering up to the wagon in assembled units. Currently, brakes are suspended from the wagon structure and therefore are affected by loading and unloading. In the case of disc brakes, this is of little consequence as they are clasping parallel cheek discs, but with tread brakes, the action of loading or unloading with the brake applied, puts excessive loads into the rigging as the blocks are forced round the wheel. In the case of pedestal suspensions, it should be possible to mount the blocks off the suspension saddle casting so that the differential movement can be eliminated. In this respect, we are investigating the most acceptable method of mounting the blocks with a view to a standard mounting arrangement. As the block would always be square to the wheel the problem of taper wear would also be eliminated. It will add to the unsprung weight but should not increase it above that presently allowed for disc brakes.

ADVANTAGES OFFERED BY COMPOSITION BLOCKS

    (a) Reduced tare weight. The higher coefficient enables simpler and lighter rigging to be utilised substantially reducing the wagon tare weight.

    (b) As lower block forces are required the force in the pins and levers is less, leading to less component wear. Estimated block life is longer than that expected for cast iron blocks.

    (c) T.B.L. Blocks do not emit sparks during braking, therefore there is less fire risk on wagons carrying flammable products.

    (d) The braking performance is at least as good as with disc brakes and substantially better than cast iron brakes.

    (e) Failure of the brake on one axle does not affect the brakes on the other axle as both axles are independently braked. This also frees the centre of the wagon for other equipment, such as hopper doors.

    (f) Should the wagon be operated with the brake applied, the resultant damage is less than that experienced with other systems.

    (g) The unsprung weight is less than with disc brakes.

    (h) The initial cost is less than with disc brakes.

CONCLUSION

We have made a great deal of progress over the last four years but more needs to be done to perfect the system. Even within our latest layout, we are constantly improving and simplifying the components, and new developments in cylinders, slack adjusters and the blocks themselves are also in hand.

However, we are confident that our latest proposals offer the lightest, least expensive and most efficient automatic brake so far fitted to air braked wagons.

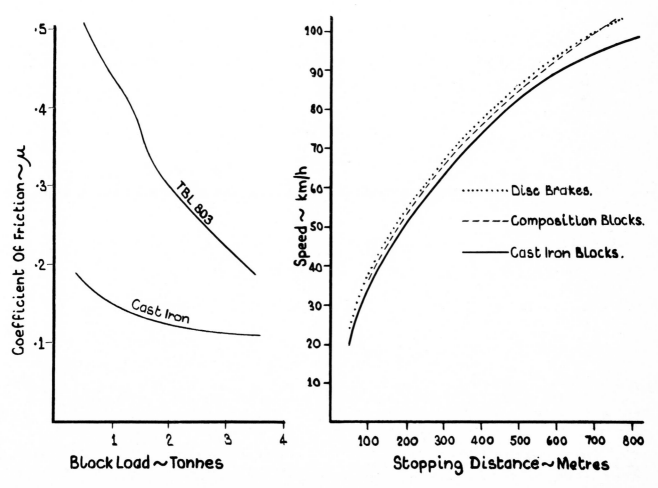

Fig 1

Fig 2

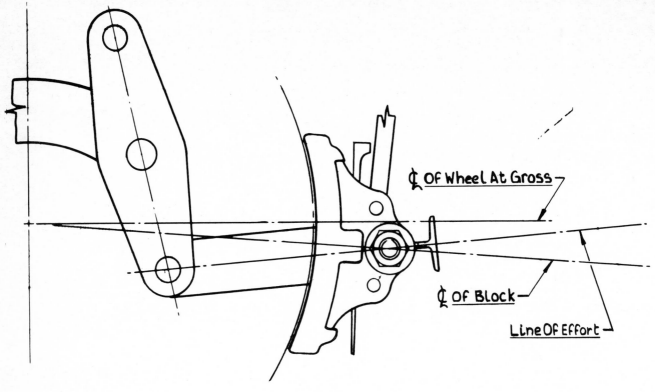

Fig 3

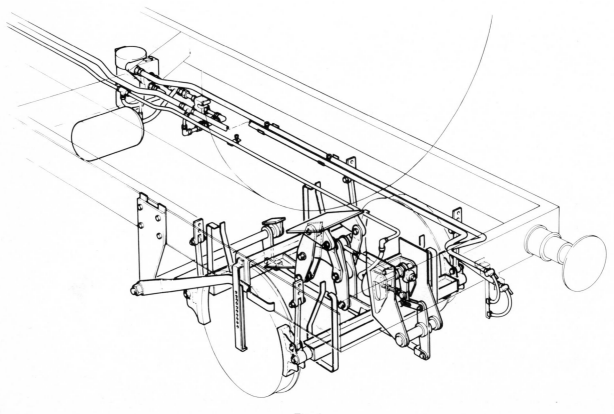

Fig 4

C34/81   © IMechE 1981

C39/81

Some points about freight wagon development on the European continent during the last ten years with special reference to the work of ORE B12 committee

N H C E ZEEVENHOOVEN
N V Nederlandse Spoorwegen

1. HISTORY AND ACTIVITIES OF ORE B12 COMMITTEE (ORE B12 committee 'Standardization of wagons').

1.1 Generalities

For those not familiar with the ORE organization, it might be useful to explain the guiding principle according to which it functions.

The ORE is essentially an institute for the exchange of technical knowledge and know-how between the member railways. The ORE itself does not carry out any research, but subsidizes technical investigations carried out on behalf of international authority; its executive bodies are expert technical committees in which - and this is very basic - no industries as such take part; industrial delegates sometimes join in as invited experts or/and as observers of industrial groups.
Technical research is in principle always sponsored through a national railway administration and money is never directly channelled to the industries concerned.

As in every set-up, this has advantages as well as disadvantages: in its favour the relative absence of industrial pressure in the committees in which the experts can speak with impartiality on the basis of personal authority

A disadvantage is the difficulty of the stimulus lacking of direct sponsored research in which industry takes a direct part and is a partner in identifying the problems and in formulating the tasks to be fulfilled.

The B12 committee has been founded early in the existence of ORE with the goal of developing standard goods wagons for the member railways. The B12 committee has gradually grown into its present major role as a permanent group which defines the principal lines of freight wagon development on the continent.
As a result the major technical subassemblies to be used on the continent are thus determined.

Its second important role[2] is the specification of standard wagons of the principal current types in use in large numbers on the major European railways.

[1] The committee's title assumes this to be the primary role.

See: Table 1 for a survey of major subassemblies sofar unified/standardized by the UIC subcommittee "wagons" in conjunction with ORE B12 committee.

Roughly speaking the B12 committee has occupied itself up to 1964 with two axle wagons and has specified in conjunction with the UIC subcommittee for wagons the major parts and subassemblies of wagons which were to be unified.

A very important subassembly thus specified was the so called double link suspension on all European 2 axle wagons applied ever since.[2] (see fig. 1 for an idea of the double link suspension).
After 1964 the committee has done much work to adapt the automatic coupler to the conception and design of freight wagons. A very important milestone was the standardization of a bogie (the so called Y25 series), apt to be used on bogie freight wagons up to speeds of 120 km/h. (see fig. 2)

After 1970 an increasing range of 4 axle freight wagons has been standardized and further important work has been done in the field of subassemblies, determining of type testing -RP 17-[4] and research in the field of important detail problems concerning springs, steel, timber floor members, plywood. (See references)

1.2 Critical approach of what has been achieved

A critical approach to the work of B12 committee so far performed leads to the following comment:

The confrontation of the best of knowledge of the wagon experts and their collaborators of the European railways has led to the birth and development of a series of wagon types, which can be considered as the best ever developed from the point of view of:

2. robustness and aptitude to the rougher aspects of railway operation. The relative low figure of the failure rate in service is witness to this statement.

[2] It is here the place to remind readers the UIC definition of the 5 stages of uniformity distinguished by UIC.
a) Normalization quality and dimensions,
b) Compatibility, c) Interchangeability,
d) Unification, e) Standardization.

2. Running qualities in relation to the developed 2 axle/double link suspension gear and the standardized 2 axle/bogies.
3. Low maintenance costs. This has lead to the possibility of doubling the inspection period from 3 to 6 years and major overhauls are only needed after 12 ÷ 16 years.

If this is all taken for granted it cannot be said that the wagons created are by definition the most economic of all possible designs from the point of production costs. This statement is maintained notwithstanding the fact that during the development of every wagon type serious efforts are made to compare alternative constructions from technical and economical points of view. A number of reasons led to the impossibility of attaining the goal of developing in a common act the most economical wagon construction.
To be mentioned are:
1. The most economical construction is a function of the production facilities present in different factories.
2. The most economical construction of a whole wagon is not necessarily the sum of the most economical constructions of the individual construction items.
3. The most economical construction is a function of time: what is economical today, does not need to be economical tomorrow.

The other activity already mentioned, undertaken under the cover of international collaboration in B12 committee and the UIC committee for wagons, has been the unification of important subassemblies; this activity has given rise to:

1. A very even performance of wagons of different railways in international traffic.
2. The possibility of mutual technical maintenance of some wagon types belonging to different railways
3. The operational possibility of pooling of wagons from different railways (creation of the pool Europ and other pools).

To this must be added that the many subassemblies unified and partly standardized are used on almost every type of wagon designed in Europe. This means that from the point of view of operational behaviour uniformity has been obtained to a large extent. As has been said it can be argued about what activity of B12 is the more important: the development of standard wagons or the specification of standard subassemblies for use on almost every type of freight wagon actually built in Europe. There is an inclination to view upon the unification/standardization and specification of subassemblies as the more important and the longer lasting activity.

The ever growing collection of UIC technical specifications -here the 500 series for the unified parts and the 800 series for the actual specification are being considered has assumed a great authority in the third world. For many enquiries addressed to European industries and elsewhere conformity of constructions to the UIC standards is required. Inversely this has lead to the fact that industry is ever more orientated on making the UIC specified parts.

So far concentration of production wagons of a given type on an international scale has failed; the concentration of production of subassemblies by relatively few specialized European industries has succeeded. The effect on spare parts policy in relation to the economy, the quantity needed and quality obtainable has been favourable. In terms of price development this is more arguable.

As fewer industries concentrate on making special items for a limited number of clients the fruits of rational production tend to favour more the concerned industries and benefit to a far lesser extent the railway administrations.
In this context it is very interesting to split up the detail costs for an average type of 2 axle and bogie wagon and evaluate the value contribution of the wagon builder and the part, which goes to the supplying industries.
See table 3 for a survey of costs split between subassemblies of a freight wagon and the wagon body with its direct accessories.

1.3 Pros and cons of the pattern of work of B12 committee

Long delays:

One of the disadvantages of the pattern of work of the ORE B12 committee and the mission performed is definitely the long delay needed to develop a new type of standardized wagon.

The principal phases are the following:

1 year – Initiative has to be taken by one or several railways; need for the concerned type of wagon on a wider international scale must be proved. (Approval by UIC 4th/5th Commission)

1 year – Specification in detail of properties of the wagons concerned; confrontation of wishes of the potential users, operating railways and of the technical, operating and commercial departments takes place. (Id.)

2 years – Standardization task confided to B12 committee. Design and constructional work of prototypes takes place. (task formulated by Control Committee of ORE)

1 year – Test service of prototypes and final modifications to standard wagon are being carried out. Complete set of manufacturing drawings is being prepared.

5 years – (Final approval by Control Committee of ORE and presentation to 4th/5th UIC Commission).

Know-how drain:

On the industrial and railway side there are unfortunately many works which possess only a skeleton drawing office, and several railways are even without any worthwhile know-how.
In fact B12 acts as a very important mediating office of

a considerable amount of know-how, assembled and transmitted by those who have the know-how to those who have not. For the railways as brother organizations this is no special negative point; for the industries the continuous flow of valuable know-how is a matter of understandable concern.

Patented constructions:

There is a strong tendency to use non patented constructions.
Although understandable from several points of view, it often leads to the choice of a less valuable design in order to avoid the difficulties —although the settlement of how to deal with patents is internationally codified at the ORE office— involved in dealing with patented constructions which in the first instance are only made by one factory. An equally negative side effect is the gradual extincton of initiatives taken by the wagon building industries to develop new constructions and improve designs as the chances of reward in terms of utilization of patented constructions is slight!

Compromise and stratification

Any effort of standardization means a compromise of some order.
This can be considered as a grave disadvantage, but might be called an acceptable feature providing standardization does not lead to stratification of the constructional development. This means that after a couple of years (not exceeding e.g. 5 years) and a fresh approach to the once standardized wagon had to be taken and eventually a redesign or even a respecification must be undertaken.

Building in large quantities

One important goal of standardization has not been reached: the building of large numbers of standardized wagons of a given type by one industry to ensure at the same time:
(a) a continuous fabrication and works occupation
(b) a high quality
(c) a cheap manufacture at low prices.

Chauvinistic purchasing policies by many railways pursued for many reasons have effectively forbidden that the real fruits of standardization could be harvested.

There is, however, an important exception to this rule and that is when international orientated companies as huge private wagon hire/leasing company order wagons or when Interfrigo and Intercontainer do the same thing. It is an ironic comment that these companies do not often order standardized constructions, but stick to the unified stage of many designs.

Possible different approach of the kind of work of B12 committee

There could be a different approach to the development of international mutually used freight wagons. This would be the so-called homologation procedure.
This idea would mean a procedure in which no effective design work would be undertaken by any ORE (B12) committee, but only very severe specifications and operating requirements were to be formulated for items and wagons developed by the industry. A complete and very elaborate programme of testing and operation would be needed and supervised by international bodies, before a homologation could be declared and thus a general use by everyone would be approved. In special cases UIC/ORE act in this way. An example is given in the international approach to pneumatic brake systems and elastic gears for the A.C.
The homologation is limited as to the fulfilment of specifications and requirements and says little of effective operational performance. No different detailed phases of service behaviour are required before the final homologation is pronounced.

In both cases homologation is not applied as a real alternative organisational system but for reasons of railway safety. In the case of braking, the history of this homologation procedure is much older than ORE.

The major advantage of a homologation procedure would be the much quicker working of the system and the possible universal application to all wagons put into service. The intricacies of international collaboration impartial judgment related to the then much more evident presence of industry in all proceedings would present themselves as a new problem. It is not too easy to foresee how such a system would work itself out, but it would be worthwhile to study the eventual merits and disadvantages.

1.4 Final conclusion

Taking an overall view of the history and performance of B12 committee certainly results in a very positive appreciation of what has been done.
The more important role seems to be the work performed on unified/standardized technical subassemblies.
The work done on standardization of general purpose wagons is nevertheless also very impressive.
Finally on the human level the presence and activities of B12 committee has given rise to an ever increasing understanding of international experts on all levels of railways as well as industries, which has contributed on an individual basis enormously to the progress of railway techniques on the freight wagon side.

Figs. 3a—3f give a full pictorial display of wagons so far standardized by ORE B12 committee.

Insofar as the elastic gear for the automatic couplers e.g. is concerned, also an additional endurance test is required to make sure a proper behaviour in real operating conditions over a long time.

2. EXAMPLE OF DEVELOPMENT: THE STANDARD 4 AXLE AND 6 AXLE COILWAGON

2.1 Generalities

The four aspect: <u>users</u>, <u>operating</u>, <u>design</u> and <u>maintenance</u>, which are to be considered if a new wagon is designed, will be illustrated on the basis of the development of the standard coilwagon.
The transport of rolled coils, warm and cold rolled ones, is in ever increasing demand on behalf of the steelindustry. Warm rolled sections and coils can be transported on open flats with either the axis or the coils positioned vertically or horizontally. Cold rolled coils however must be transported under cover and preferably, because of their fragile nature, with the axis horizontally and positioned in berths.

The major types available are: sliding roof and hood wagons. Because of the ever larger coil sizes, <u>the sliding roof</u> wagon represents no longer a logical solution, because the crane pincers during loading and unloading operations can no longer be accommodated between the walls of sliding roof wagons.
From the point of view of the <u>user</u> only <u>a hood wagon</u> is acceptable.
Because of the absolute condition to secure an impeccable tightness of the hoods from the railway <u>operating</u> point of view only a system with rigid hoods is possible. This system makes the loading and unloading more delicate, because much manoeuvring of hoods is needed to free all the parts of the wagon consecutively. This feature is thus not a wish of the user, but a consequence of the delicate load.

2.2 Development of chosen coilwagon types

After prolonged discussion on an international basis it was thus decided to standardize the hood wagon instead of a sliding roof wagon.
After careful consideration from the users and operating points no general purpose wagon was chosen, but a specialized coilwagon was suggested. A wagon equally suited for the transport of bars would have been longer and even more fragile in its concept.

As indicated above this decision was based on the increasing number of heavy and relatively large coils of up to 45 tons to be transported.
It is ironic that the present development of the coil sizes shows a tendency towards very large diameters of rather small width (relationship width/diameter: $< 0,4$), and consequently less mass.

And until recently even more unfavourable the so-called 'C' hook.
Fragile because no fixed end fronts could have been chosen. A larger number of hoods (4) would have been needed to free a sufficient length of the wagon for the possibility of loaded bars. The berths must in the latter case be 'filled' in with correspondingly shaped parts.

Table 5 gives an indication of a possible load scheme of the developed wagons.

From the <u>users</u> point the length of wagon destined to transport heavy goods and called upon to be shunted in restricted factory areas must, for the max. permissible axle load (= 20 tons for the time being, and 22 tons in due course on certain mainlines) be as short as possible.
To ensure a freedom as large as possible -<u>operating</u> requirement- the four-axle and and more general purpose wagon has been designed for C3 (=7.2t/m) and the more special 6 axle wagon is designed for C4 (= 8 t/m).
The constructional <u>design</u> of the wagon was taken up by a working group inside B12 committee with the assistance of three major wagon builders, Arbel France and Linke Hoffmann Germany for the 4 axle wagon and Talbot Germany for the 6 axle wagon.
The design was inspired by a type already developed by Arbel for the SNCF.
It is interesting to give a short idea of some principal points of the design of the 4 axle wagon.

- three hooded system with mutual interlocking (fig. 4)
- simple end locking (fig. 5)
- underframe design in the vicinity of the bogies "gooseneck design" (fig. 6)

- guiding device (forks) for stabilizing the position of coils during transport (fig. 7)

- careful choice of the gradient of the berths to enable impact shocks to be taken up without damage to the coils and danger to the wagon.
A consecutive gradient combination $30^\circ/45^\circ$ has been chosen to limit the wagon length for a given number of berths (fig. 8).

As the most perfect design has its flaws an operating experience is needed to correct design and to solve manufacturing defects.
The following points have consequently been corrected:

- Supports of the berth stabilizers have been improved together with better accessibility for conservation purposes.
- A still better gooseneck shape.
- Improvements have been made to the hoods to comply with all requirements of personal safety during handling.
- Improvements have been made to obtain better tightness of the hood seals in wintery conditions.

It is perfectly clear that the more careful the design is, the more <u>maintenance</u> -free the ultimate resulting wagon is. Of course this statement is only true as an optimum goal. It is quite clear from the start that a given type of wagon possesses by definition some delicate points, which, as many items, give rise to special maintenance care.
In the case of the coil wagon are to be mentioned: the hoods.
Whatever conception the hoods have, they remain very vulnerable to damage during loading and unloading operations. The latest developments tend to favour light simple

constructions with the aptitude of repairs on the spot.

Judgement has also not been uniform on the relative merits of steel, alu or plastic hood construction; either variants are thus admitted.

A very important point has been the fitting of class C buffers, allowed for 15 km/h impact shocks to be taken for an end force not exceeding 1300 kN pro buffer.

Standard Y25 bogies have been specified from the start.

2.3 Critical evaluation

To define a unified/standard wagon for international use, means always a compromise in terms of usage. It is extremely difficult to balance pros and cons in the kind of comparison where a more general purpose and a special purpose wagon alternative are involved.

To be distinguished are:
- general purpose wagon = wagon apt to transport many kinds of goods: a special adaptation is required to tranport special goods.
- multipurpose wagon = wagon adapted to transport a whole category of goods.
- special purpose wagon = wagon specially fitted for a very limited range of goods.

The ORE coilwagon is an example of the last kind.

In the final balance one must enter:

(a) the number of special purpose wagons required
(b) the usage criterion in terms of idling times of the special wagon type against:

the better usage intensity but also higher operating costs of general purpose wagons.

See table 5 for the conflicting interests of users, operating, maintenance and design.

As said before the combination of design efforts of many railway administrations and industries involved lead to a much better product than was possible ever before. Design and maintenance costs are thus optimized, the price of construction only to a very limited extent.

If the maximum loaded mass remains 80 tons the Y25 bogie will be adequate to its task. A rise to 88 tons will call for a reinforced version or an alternative design.

The wagons (braking and bogie) are adapted to a max. speed of 100 km/h in loaded position, but the wagons can be sent back empty in fast trains running up to 120 km/h.

It is hoped that in this short context an idea is given of the considerations given for development of a major special type of 4 axle freight wagon for UIC member railways.

Some dates, as final illustration of the work accomplished:

1967 first initiative on behalf of Netherlands Railways.
1969 result of discussion within B12 sent to the 'group ad hoc bogie wagons' of UIC
1971 Programme approved by UIC of different types of 4 axle wagons to be standardized.
1973 4 axle coilwagon unified and introduced in UIC leaflet 571.
1974 Start of design work and building of prototype standard 4 axle coilwagon (constructional detailing and building)
1976 Prototype ready.
1978 Final report approved by the ORE control committee.

3. MAJOR DESIGN PARAMETERS AND THE RELATIVE IMPORTANCE OF DISTINCTIVE FIGURES IN RAILWAY WAGON DESIGN

3.1 Generalities

The determining parameters and limits in the design of UIC FREIGHT WAGONS ARE:

I Major parameters

1. Permissible axle load for bulk load wagons	20 t up to 120 km/h, 22 t considered
2. The max. permissible value for t/m	C2 : 6,4 t/m - more or less generally accepted C3 : 7,2 t/m C4 : 8 t/m limits especially important for bulk wagons: desired load cat. dependent on type of bulk goods transported.
3. The max. permitted distance between axles/bogies	9 m : two axle wagons 17,5 m: between consecutive axles of bogie wagons (N.B. this means 19,3 between bogie centres)
4. The buffing height	950 ÷ 1045 mm (range to be respected for the future automatic coupler).
5. The max. field of action of the automatic coupler	≤ 220 mm (requirement to couple in the transition point of a 135 m curve and straight track). (UIC leaflet 530)
6. The (kinematic) loading gauge	As defined in UIC leaflet 505-3 for wagons.
7. Minimum curves	35 m: 2 axle wagons

60 m: bogie wa-
gons

8. The limits set on the geometry and empty mass from the point of view of security against derailment

according to a calculating scheme set up by ORE B125 committee new wagons must be able to with-stand a 600 kN longitudinal for-ce without ten-dency to derail-ment in a transi-tion point of a curve with radius 135 m, and straight track coupled between a two axle open wa-gon on one end and a 4 axle flat on the other end.

II <u>Secondary design limits are:</u>

a. The minimum inside width of covered wa-gons   2600 mm

b. The minimum inside width of refrigera-ted wagons   2500 mm

c. The minimum free height of the door opening in a covered wagon   2050 mm

d. The standard width of a container wagon   8' (eventually 2500 mm)

e. The minimum gradients to be respected in self-discharging wa-gons as a function of the transported bulk goods etc.

3.2 <u>Relative influence on the different kind of wagons</u>

Generally speaking covered wagons be they:
(a) normal covered wagons with one or two sets of doors
(b) sliding door wagons
(c) refrigerated wagons
the surface or/and volume and therefore the max. permitted length becomes the deciding parameter for a given width and height.
The length is further limited by conside-rations of derailment safety in relation with the parameters:

(a) length
(b) length over linking pins of the A.C /axle distance or bogie distance ('c/a') (especially important for 2 axle wagons)
(c) empty mass.

In fact the factors I1, I3, I4, I5, I6, I8
                 IIa, b, c
play a determining role.

In the same context for bulk wagons be it:
(a) mineral/coal wagons
(b) tank wagons
the value t/m is the most deciding parameter.

In fact the factors I1, I2,
               IId
play a determining role.

3.3 <u>Distinguished figures used</u>

In the next paragraphs the following dis-tinguished figures are used:
wagon parameter: t/m[*] of length
                  t/m of useful loading length
                  t/m^2 useful mass
                  t/m^3 useful mass
track parameter: axle 'load' in tons, t/m: total mass/m length.

3.4 <u>Possible modifications of existing rules as outlined above</u>

The relative merits of changing the axle load - determining factor common to all types of wagon- are briefly explained at the end of this chapter based on a report esta-blished by the SNCF. See the principal conclusions appendix 1.
The possibilities of extending the classifi-cation C with a fifth class C5 (8.8 t/m) are only given for a limited number of routes, where bridges built according to the UIC ru-les as laid down in the concerned leaflet are omni-present.

A further extension of the max. distance of 17.5 m between consecutive axles is to be ruled out as signalling circuits on open track and in major shunting yards are based on this limit.
The same is true for any modification of the buffing height.

The recently defined kinematic loading gauge in leaflet 505-3 can only be modified for distinguished routes, where a more generous gauge is being pursued.
The most likely future gauge is then the alternative C2 defined in the special wor-king group.
Any modification of derailment rules in the sense of lower permissible figures is not to be expected as ever longer, heavier and fas-ter trains are introduced.

3.5 <u>Consequences of present limits</u>

Based on a limited axle load of 20 t for all wagons except bulk wagons the scope of the parameter empty mass/unit of length between head stocks is: 1 ÷ 1.15 for 2 axle; 1.3 ÷ 1.4 for 4 axle.

The max. useful length (= headstock length - end walls) for a given standard wagon of all types can be expressed as:

[*] 'tons' in terms of tare mass, useful load mass and total mass.

c/a 2a + 0,5 . 2a + 2 . 1025 -

   distance between   length shaft
   axles: 9000   A.C. (Aut.
                                Coupler)

2 . 620 - 100

   length of   thickness of
   one buffer   end walls

The max. equivalent length of a bogie wagon can be expressed as:

$$2a + 2 . (1475 \div 1675) + 2 . 1025$$

underbrace $= $ overhang

$$- 2 . 620 - 100.$$

Overhang: 2500 ÷ 2700 mm
N.B. limited by the possibilities of UIC
     leaflets 530-1 and 2.

2a = distance between bogies ⩽ 19.300 mm.

N.B. As a matter of fact the coupling plane of the A.C. is 0,0025 m ahead of the buffer plane.

Covered wagons:

In appendix 2 is indicated that the max. possible length of
2 axle wagons is: 15.550 mm
4 axle wagons is: 22.500 mm
for a given range of specific surface loadings

    between 0.4 and 1 t/m^2 - covered
                                   wagons
    between 0.4 and 0.8 t/m^2 - refrigerating wagons
    between 0.4 and 1.4 t/m^2 - container wagons

The equivalent range of specific volume loadings is for all types of wagons taken between 0.2 and 0.6 t/m^3.

In appendix 3 is the tare mass calculated as a function of length for three different types of wagons against the max. possible lengths.
From the diagrams presented the following can be derived:
if surface loading is dominant:
2 axle covered wagon T.l. ≅ 15500 mm:
covered ~ 0.7 ÷ 1 t/m^2
4 axle covered wagon T.l. ≅ 21300 mm:
covered < 1 t/m^2
2 axle refrigerated wagon T.l. ≅ 15500 mm: covered 0.75 ÷ 1 t/m^2
4 axle refrigerated wagon T.l. ≅ 24000 mm: covered 0.8 t/m^2 (22500 longest wagon permitted)

If Vol. loading is dominant:
2 axle covered wagon T.l. = 15500 mm:
covered: ~ 0,3 ÷ 0.6 t/m^3
4 axle covered wagon T.l. ≅ 17300 mm:
covered: < 0.6 t/m^3
2 axle refrigerated wagon T.l. ≅ 15500 mm: covered 0.35 ÷ 0,6 t/m^3
4 axle refrigerated wagon T.l. ≅ 18300 mm: covered: 0,6 t/m^3

Bulk wagons:

The determining parameter is the t/m value. The axle load is varied between 20 and 22 tons and the t/m values are varied from 8 to 8.8 t/m.
As an example the Fad type of wagon -self-discharging wagon type for massive, immediate discharge is taken.
Taking the non useful length of three representative wagons off:
- length of buffers
- serving platforms.

In the design of such a type of wagon deciding points are the permissible length of the trap.: ⩽ 5000 mm, the gradient of the bulk reservoir and the specific mass values of the bulk loads to be transported.

Basically there are two alternative designs: in the first design two bulk reservoirs are joined in one wagon, in the second a wagon carries only one and two such wagons are shortcoupled. See fig. 10 .

The useful volume per m of wagon length is
   Wagontype 1.   75 m^3
             2.   80 m^3
             3.   60 m^3
      4a/b. 2 x 38/20.5

See fig. 11 for the most important parameters of these wagons.
It is clear from the presentation that the problem for bulk wagons is essentially a problem of the number of axles; it is perhaps amazing, but there is no absolute relationship between the t/m values and the permissible axle load.

For transport of lighter bulk goods, e.g. cokes, the 4 axle 75 and 80 m^3 wagons are optimal; for transport of minerals as iron on either the 6 axle or 8 axle wagons come into their own.

4. FUTURE PATTERNS OF FREIGHT WORKING AND RELATIVE ENERGY EFFICIENCY

4.1 Generalities:

In the light of energy conservation the railways can present their inherent advantages related to the rolling of steel wheels on steel rails.

Further substantial improvements can only be scored in the following terms:
(a) to operate longer trains
(b) to limit the max. speed of freight trains to values which do not exceed those absolutely necessary to run a mixed passenger/freight service on the same tracks for a given needed line capacity
(c) to run eventually more night freight on electrified lines.

The design of lighter freight wagons can only contribute marginally to energy saving of total freight operation.

4.2 Future pattern

Providing firstly that apart from government measures taken to create better starting conditions for competition between rail and road no direct stimulating regulations are proclaimed and assuming secondly that the railways do a real effort to improve the position where their strength is most obvious a pattern of development as indicated below could be imagined:

The strong market sectors for the railways are:

- Whenever the quantities allow this and the demand of transport permits the operation of blocktrains or trains composed of wagon groups, the use of the railway must logically be an economic proposition. This kind of traffic is to be found in the transport of basic materials, minerals, chemicals, coal and mineral oils of all kinds.
- A more special role of the railways is possible as transport link in a production chain, where the production is geographically split.
  Here again the regular pattern of the traffic even of moderate streams of goods is very suited to railway traffic.
- Combined transport operations be they: piggy back operation, ISO container or road/rail interchange container casings traffic are definitely a field of potential growth for the railways.
- Transport of specialized freight: food products in refrigerated condition; dangerous goods in the form of dangerous chemicals or nuclear waste.

On the other hand individual wagon load will further decline, considered in terms of relative importance.

As a consequence of the tendencies outlined above the number of specialized and for the most part bogie wagons will further increase.
An exception will be the transport of voluminous goods for which 2 axle wagons come into consideration.
Every endeavour to improve sharply the average annual kilometrage per wagon will mean an almost proportional diminution of the present wagon fleet. It is to be expected that the total fleet will certainly shrink to half the present size.

The special purpose wagons needed are very robust and not too light to allow long maintenance bridging periods.

The max. speed of the average freight will not exceed 100 km/h with the possible exception of container and similar trains; block trains will stick to max. speeds of 80 km/h.

Speaking of the possibility of increasing mass and length of freight trains in the dense pattern of passenger trains on the average European main line and taking into account the relatively moderate distances prevailing in Europe the maximum sensible values will be in the order of:

4000 ÷ 5000 t mineral block trains, length train 600 ÷ 750 m, max. speed 80 km/h.
2000 t mixed freight trains, length train < 600 m, max. speed 80 km/h.
1400 t fast freights, length < 600 m, max. speed 100 km/h.
1000 ÷ 1200 t container trains, length < 600 m, max. speed 120 km/h.

*) only possible if wagons equipped with strengthened elastic draw gear system.

**) only possible if wagons equipped with strengthened elastic buff and draw gear system.

Even after the introduction of the automatic coupler it is not to be expected that masses will be appreciably bigger. The reasons for this are the following:

1 To handle general merchandise trains of bigger masses than around 2000 t ask for enormous locomotive powers, which are not too economic to build and operate.
2 Line capacity is badly influenced by too heavy trains, acceleration is low even with high powers installed.
3 Energy supply on electric lines becomes un-economic if large demands for a limited time are asked for.
4 The limited distances in Europe ask for relatively frequent trains; traffic streams are certainly not so heavy that for a given minimum frequency still heavier masses are called for.

Energy consumption for freight trains varies widely with the type of train. Fig. 12 gives the energy consumption for acceleration of 4 different types of trains to their normal end speed.*)
Table 6 gives the energy consumption at different cruising speeds and for varied tare values of the wagons used.

As a general conclusion the statement might be valid:
Speed is the predominant parameter on energy consumption; tare has only marginal influence on operation of lines in the plane

*) Energy consumption calculated at the substation for a 1500 Volt catenary.

Appendix 1

Short summary of results of SNCF study on the merits of 22 t axle loads
(study prepared in Nov. 1976 and submitted to the UIC subcommission for permissible loads in Jan. 1977).

Suppositions made
1. 22 t axle loads only permitted on routes where no special measures to bridges and civil works have to be taken; the track must be apt to sure 22 tons axle loads.
2. 22 t axle loads only applied to bogie wagons circulating in block trains.

3. Raise of tare mass and price proportionally to higher axle load.

Marginal additional maintenance costs:
(a) proportional to the product of hauled brute ton km multiplied with (average of all axle loads over a given stretch)^2 as concerns the pure track replacement materials:
(b) proportional to the hauled brute ton km as concerns miscellaneous costs of track and bridges
(c) automatic coupler was considered to be in service (N.B. This had only consequences as far as the additional mass of the coupler and the equivalent loss of useful mass is concerned).

In fact only immatriculated P-wagons on the SNCF network (tank wagons, mineral wagons, general bulk load wagons of all types) come into the picture for extension of their permissible axle load, in all about 10% of the whole

Cost benefit studies showed that only block train wagons with a utilisation factor of at least 30%[a] could justify their axle loads being raised to 22 t. With lower factors the larger tare mass (by roughly 0,5 ÷ 1 t) cannot offset the higher costs of moving most of the time these larger tare masses.

Under the stated propositions a marginal benefit of admitting larger axle loads than 20 t could be proved.

The essential conclusion of this study is:

Any rise of the axle load limits over the present more or less generalised value of 20 tons should be limited to selected routes with heavy bulk traffic. The wagons apt for these higher axle loads should be 4 axle wagons with utilisation factors in heavy traffic of at least 30 but preferably 50%.

[a]Average for railway owned vehicles is in the order of 10 ÷ 15%!

Appendix 2

Max. possible wagon length

2 axle wagons

covered wagons

Max. half width at 3385 mm above rails:

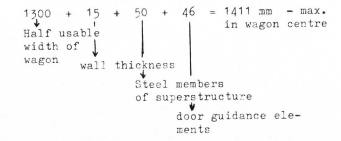

1300 + 15 + 50 + 46 = 1411 mm - max. in wagon centre
Half usable width of wagon
wall thickness
Steel members of superstructure
door guidance elements

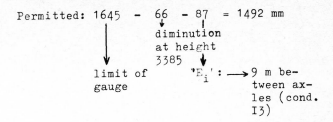

Permitted: 1645 - 66 - 87 = 1492 mm
diminution at height 3385
limit of gauge
'E_i': →9 m between axles (cond. I3)

Max overhang and thus max. wagon length is determined by conditions I5, I7 and I8 (chapter 3.2) and becomes: practical total wagon length (T.1.)

9000 + 0.5 . 9000 + 2 . 1025 = $\boxed{15.550 \text{ mm}}$

(c/a ≤ 1,5)

4 axle wagons

covered wagons

Max. half width at 3385 mm above rails

1300 + 15 + 50 + 46 = 1411 - max. in wagon centre.

Permitted: 1645 - 66 - 164 = 1415 mm
'E_i' →19300 between bogie centres (cond. I3)

Max. overhang and thus max. wagon length is again determined by conditions I5, I7 and I8 (chapter 3.2) and becomes: practical total wagon length (=T.1):

17.500[a] + 2 . 1475[a] + 2 . 1025 = $\boxed{22.500 \text{ mm}}$

[a]In relation with a minimum overhang of 2500 mm, the scope of the automatic coupler the max. distance between bogies can effectively not become larger than 17.500 mm.

Leaflet 530-1 permits in fact:

2a = 17500	overhang:	2500 mm
2a = 18500	" :	2000 mm
2a = 19300	" :	1250 mm

minimum possible overhang = 2500 mm

Appendix 3

Limits of parameters t/m^2 and t/m^3 usable load as a function of wagon length of 2 and 4 axle wagons.

Covered wagons

2 axle   4 axle (bogie)

usable internal width
2600 mm.
usable internal height
2185 mm.

relation between Usable length and actual wagon length.

U.l. = x - 1240 - 100   (x = Total length)
buffers
end wall thickness

tare mass/m length

2 axle	4 axle
1.0 t/m	1.3 t/m

formulae

$$t/m^2 \to \frac{40 - x \cdot 1,0}{2,6 \cdot (x - 1,34)}$$

$(= A_1)$

$$t/m^3 \to A_1/2.185$$

$$\frac{80 - x \cdot 1,3}{2,6 \cdot (x - 1,34)}$$

$(= A_2)$

$$A_2/2.185$$

Refrigerated wagons

2 axle	4 axle

usable internal width 2500 mm
usable internal height 2185 mm.

U.l. = x − 1240 − 200
↓
buffers   ↓
       end
    wall thick-
       ness

U.l. = x − 1240 −
       200 − 1200

− 1000
↓
ice bunkers

tare mass/m length

2 axle	4 axle
1.1 t/m	1.44 t/m

$$t/m^2 \to \frac{40 - x \cdot 1,1}{2,5 \cdot (x - 2,44)}$$

$(= B_1/2.185$

$$t/m^3 \to B_1$$

$$\frac{80 - x \cdot 1,44}{2,4 \cdot (x - 2,64)}$$

$(= B_2)$

$$B_2/2.185$$

REFERENCES

Some of the principal reports in the history of B12 are:

(1) 1956   Report on the results of the international contest on the development of open wagons: RP 2.

(2) 1962/1964   Report on the adaptation of the unified wagon types to the automatic coupler: RP 8, 9.

(3) 1967   Report on the standardization of a 2 axle bogie: RP 14.

(4) 1971   Report on tests and criteria to be applied to new type wagons: RP 17.

'Rapport Partiel' (Partiel Report)

(5) Special mention should be made of the technical document D.T. nr. 85 which defines all the major parts on the front ends of wagons. See table 2 for the major characteristics of the standard/unified wagons.

Table 1

Major parts unified/standardized sofar by UIC

UIC leaflet	Unified items	Standardized items (S)
510-1/2	Running gear	S
514	Roller bearings + axle boxes	-
517	Suspension for 2 axled wagons	S
520/21	Draw gear	-
522	Automatic couplers	
524	Elastic draw gear	-
	automatic couplers	
526	Buffers	-
527-1/2		
529	Shock-absorbing gear	-
530-1/2	Constructional details of	
	wagon parts in relation	
	to the application of the	
	automatic couplers	
535-1/2/3	Accessories to wagons as	partly S
	steps, supports, manoeuvring	
	gear of the automatic couplers.	
	Cross platforms, towing hooks	
541-1/3	Constructional details of	partly S
	pneumatic parts of brake	
	equipment	
542	Interchangeability of mecha-	-
	nical brake parts	
541-4	Brake blocks	-
570	List of different interchan-	
	geable parts	
578	Interchangeable 'stanchions'	S
590	Technical requirements for	-
	small containers	
592	Technical requirements for	S
	ISO and land containers	
593	Technical requirements for	-
	privately owned ISO and land	
	containers	

Table 2

Type of wagon	Tare mass (ton)	Length over buffers (m)	Distance between axles/bogies j' (m)	Distance between axles/bogies (m)	Usable surface open and covered wagons (m²)	Usable volume covered wagons (m³)	loaded mass/usable surface (ton/m²)	loaded mass/usable volume (ton/m³)	Pallets 800×1200	Pallets 800×1200	Pallets 1000×1200	Transported mass 20 t (ton)	Transported mass 22 t (ton)	Total mass 20 t (ton)	Total mass 22 t (ton)
2 axle															
1 normal covered wagon (G) Type 1	14,0	14,02	8,0	–	55	80	0,788	0,325				1,85	2,14	2,85	3,14
2 Type 2	12,0	10,58	5,7	–	25	60	1,120	0,467				2,65	3,03	3,78	4,16
Type 3	14,5	14,02	8,0	–	28	66	0,911	0,386				1,82	2,10	2,85	3,14
3 normal open wagon (E)	11,0	10,00	5,4	–	24	36	1,208	0,806				2,90	3,30	4,00	4,40
normal flat wagon (K)	12,5	13,86	8,0	–	35	–	0,786	–				1,98	2,27	2,89	3,17
flat multipurpose wagon (Kbs)	13,0	13,86	8,0	–	36	28,5	0,750	0,947				1,95	2,24	2,89	3,17
4 axle															
normal covered wagon (Gas(s)) Fig. 1.3.1	23,0	16,52	–	11,48		105	1,425	0,543	24	24	16	3,45	3,93	4,84	5,33
normal covered wagon (Gabs(s)) 1.3.2	29,0	21,70	–	16,66		137	0,962	0,372	20 [7]	[7]	16	2,35	2,72	3,69	4,06
normal open wagon (Eas/Eaos)	22,0	14,04	–	9,00		71	1,657	0,817				4,13	4,70	5,70	6,27
normal flat wagon (Rs/Res) 1.3.3	24,0	19,90	–	14,86		–	1,098	–				2,81	3,22	4,02	4,42
normal flat wagon (Rmms/Remms)	22,5	14,04	–	9,00		–	1,643	–				4,10	4,67	5,70	6,27
2 axle															
refrigerating wagon (Ibbs)	15,5	14,02	8,0	–		52,7 [3]	0,907	0,465 [3]	24	24	16	1,75	2,03	2,85	3,14
refrigerating wagon (Ibfs)	15,5	14,02	8,0	–		44,9 [3]	1,065	0,546 [3]	20 [7]		16	1,75	2,03	2,85	3,14
4 axle															
refrigerating wagon (Ias) Type 1 1.3.4	31,0	21,04	–	15,80	41,8	81,5 [3]	1,172	0,601 [3]	38	39	26	2,35	2,71	3,80	4,18
Type 2	32,0	22,24	–	16,80	45	87,8 [3]	1,067	0,547 [3]	40	42	28	2,16	2,52	3,60	3,96
2 axle															
4 mech. refrigerating wagon (Ibbgs)	18,5	14,02	8,0	–	28	54,6 [3]	0,768	0,394 [3]	24	24	16	1,53	1,82	2,85	3,14
mech. refrigerating wagon (Ibfgs)	18,5	14,02	3,0	–	23,5	45,8 [3]	0,915	0,469 [3]	20 [7]		16	1,53	1,82	2,85	3,14
4 axle															
mech. refrigerating wagon (Iags) Type 1	35,0	21,04	–	15,80	43	83,9 [3]	1,047	0,536 [3]	38	39	26	2,14	2,52	3,80	4,18
Type 2	36,0	22,24	–	16,80	46	89,7 [3]	0,957	0,491 [3]	42	42	28	1,98	2,34	3,60	3,96
wagon with opening roof (Taes)	24,0	14,04	9,00 [7]	–	33	74	1,697	0,757 [3]				3,99	4,56	5,70	6,27
wagon for autotransport (Laaes)	30,0	27,00	22,50 [5]	–	–	–	– [6]	– [6]				–	–	–	–
3 axle															
wagon for autotransport (Laes)	27,0	27,00	10,4 [5] / 21,00	–	–	–	– [6]	– [6]				–	–	–	–
2 axle															
selfdischarging wagon (Eds)	13,0	9,64	6,0	–	–	40	–	0,675				2,80	3,22	4,15	4,56
selfdischarging wagon with opening roof (Tds)	13,5	9,64	6,0	–	–	38	–	0,697				2,75	3,16	4,15	4,56

40

Table 2 cont.

(Continuation)	Tare mass (ton)	Length over buffers (m)	Distance between axles/bogies [1] (m)	Usable surface open face and covered wagons (m²)	Usable volume covered wagons (m³)	Characteristic figures (20 t max axle load) [9]		Number of pallets /usable surface (only for covered wagons, sliding door and refrigerating wagons) [2]			Transported mass per m. of train length		Total mass per m. of train length	
						loaded mass/usable surface (ton/m²)	loaded mass/usable volume (ton/m³)	800 x 1200 □	800 x 1200 ▭	1000 x 1200 ▭	20 t (ton)	22 t (ton)	20 t (ton)	22 t (ton)
4 axle														
sliding door wagon (Habis(s)) fig. 1.3.5	29,0	21,70	-	50	131	1,020	0,389	44	45	30	2,35	2,72	3,69	4,06
coil wagon (Shis) 1.3.6	22,5	12,04	7,00	-	-	-	-							
6 axle														
coil wagon (Sahis)	33,0	15,00	8,00	-	-	-	-							
4 axle														
selfdischarging wagon (Fads)	25,0	12,54	7,50	-	75	-	0,733				4,39	5,02	6,38	7,02
selfdischarging wagon with opening roof (Tads)	25,5	12,54	7,50	-	71,5	-	0,762				4,35	4,98	6,38	7,02
containerwagon (Lgmss)	18,0	15,79	10,75	-	-	-	-				3,93)[6]		5,06	
containerwagon with shock absorber (Lgjkkmmss)	18,0	16,34	11,30	-	-	-	-				3,64		4,72	
containerwagon (Lgss)	18,0	19,64	14,60	-	-	-	-				3,16		4,07	
containerwagon with shock absorber (Lgjss)	23,0	21,00	15,80	-	-	-	-				2,71		3,81	
6 axle														
containerwagon (Loggss)	27,0	27,10	10,70.2	-	-	-	-				3,43		4,43	

[1] Distance between pivot centres.

[2] 800 x 1200 mm: introduction possible over both sides; 1000 x 1200 introduction only possible over the long side.

[3] Usable volume = usable surface x h (supposed 1,95 m).

[4] 9 m = distance between 2 axles; 22,5 m = distance between extreme axles.

[5] 10,4 m = distance between extreme axles and center axle; 21 m = distance between extreme axles.

[6] Depending on the cars to be transported.

[7] One range in longitudinal direction and one range in transversal direction.

[8] Calculated with 850 x 850 and 1050 x 1250 mm in connection with an eventual overhang and improperly placed the pallets.

[9] For coil and selfdischarging wagons the geometric surface between headstocks is taken.

[10] Container mass included.

Table 3

Split of constructional costs of a given type of a 2 axle and a bogie wagon.

	Sliding door wagon 2 axle	Self-discharging wagon 4 axle (controlled discharge)
Wagonbody inclusive door and mechanism, + minor parts (steps, supports etc.)	62%	x
Wagonbody inclusive traps and mechanism + minor parts (steps, supports etc.)	x	50,5%
Buff and draw gear (buffers, ecrew couplers + elastic element)	6,5%	4 %
Pneumatic brake parts	13%	8%
Mechanical brake parts mounted under the wagon body		
Bogie frame:	x	37,5%
Springs	x	
Brake rigging	x	
Wheels + bearing	x	
Double link suspension:	} 17%	
Springs		x
Double links		x
Axle guards		x
Wheel + bearings		x

Table 4

Illustration and summary of different options of users, operators, maintenance and design.

Matrix of conflicting requirements.

	Consequences
Users ask for special purpose wagon:	expensive, complex, freight well protected.
Operating asks for general purpose wagon:	cheap, simple, freight not well protected eventually higher mileage than special purpose wagons.
Maintenance asks for general purpose wagon:	easy to maintain complex for reasons of absence of fixation equipment and facilities for easy loading/ unloading.
Design asks for special wagon:	easier to design, robust constructions possible.

Table 5

Principal characteristics of the coil wagon

	4 axle wagon	6 axle wagon
Length	12,04	15,0 m
U.l.[a]	10,8 m	13,76 m
U.W.[b] over berths	2,3 ÷ 2,4 m	2,3 ÷ 2,4 m
Distance between bogies	7,0 m	8,0 m
Distance of axles in bogie	1,8 m	1,7 m
Tare mass	22,5 t	33 t
Berth	Coil ∅	Coil ∅
1	1000 ÷ 2250 mm	1200 ÷ 2250 mm
2	800 ÷ 1700	1200 ÷ 2700
3	1000 ÷ 2700	1200 ÷ 2700
4	800 ÷ 1700	1200 ÷ 2700
5	1000 ÷ 2250	1200 ÷ 2250

[a] U.L. = usable length

[b] U.W. = Usable width

Survey of loading variants in terms of mass

	4 axle 20t/axles					6 axle 20t/axle				
	1	2	3	4	5	1	2	3	4	5
a.			45t				43,5		43,5	
b.	29				29	29		29		29
c.	19,5		19,5		19,5	21,75	21,75		21,75	21,75
d.	14,5	14,5		14,5	14,5	17,4	17,4	17,4	17,4	17,4
e.	11,5	11,5	11,5	11,5	11,5					
Tech. Max.	33	17	45	17	33	33	45	45	45	33

Table 6

Energy consumption of four categories of feight trains at
different cruising speeds and varying tare values.

			kWh/km	kWh/km/t	Speed
I	mixed freight	1600 t	41	0,0256	80 km/h
	(less tare mass)	1550 t	39,7 (- 3%)	0,0248 (-3%)	80 km/h
			29 (- 29%)	0,018 (- 29%)	60 km/h
			52,8 (+ 29%)	0,033 (+ 29%)	100 km/h
II	mineral	2400 t	35	0,0146	80 km/h
	(less tare mass)	2370 t	34,56 (- 1%)	0,0144 (- 1%)	80 km/h
			26 (- 26%)	0,011 (- 26%)	60 km/h
			45,3 (+ 29%)	0,0189 (+ 29%)	100 km/h
III	container	1200 t	45	0,0375	100 km/h
	(less tare mass)	1150 t	43 (- 4%)	0,036 (- 4%)	100 km/h
			33 (- 27%)	0,0275 (- 27%)	80 km/h
			46,1 (+ 2,4%)	0,0384 (+ 2,4%)	102,5 km/h
IV	empty mineral	750 t	35	0,0466	100 km/h
	(less tare mass)	700 t	33 (- 7%)	0,043 (- 7%)	100 km/h
			24 (-21,5%)	0,032 (- 21,5%)	80 km/h
			38,3 (+ 9,4%)	0,051 (+ 9,4%)	111,6 km/h

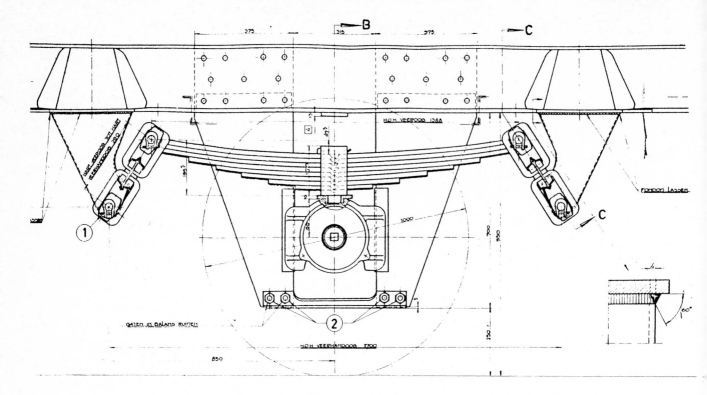

Fig 1   Double link suspension as standard for 2 axle wagons

Fig 2   Y25 standard bogie

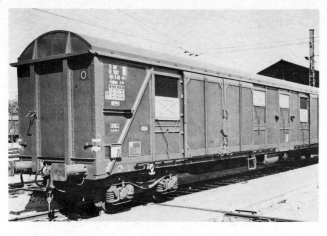
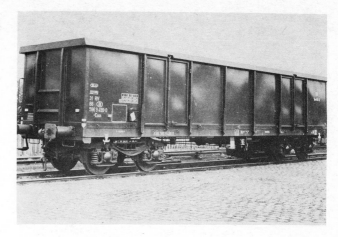
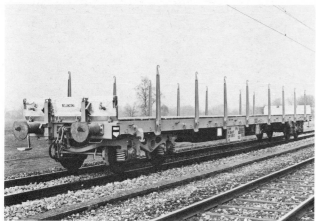

Fig 3   Major standardized/unified freight wagons: since the start of B12

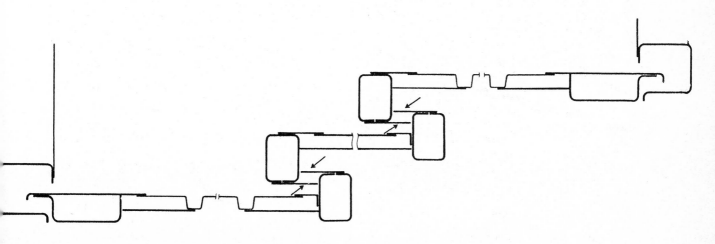

Fig 4   Mutual interlocked hoods

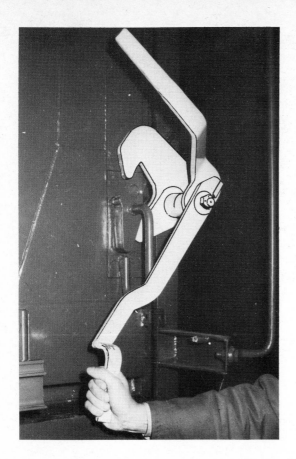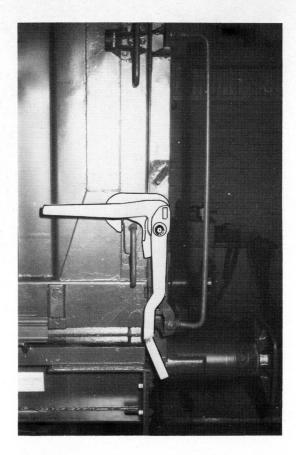

Fig 5   Simple end lock

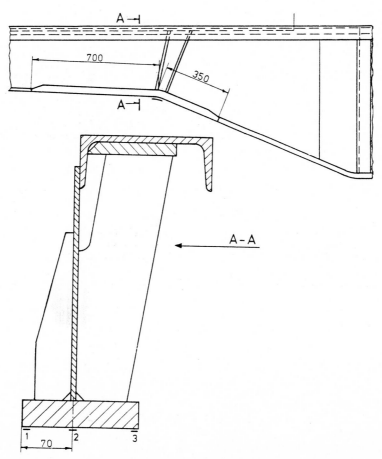

Fig 6   'Gooseneck' underframe

Fig 7 Displacement bogie of the hoods

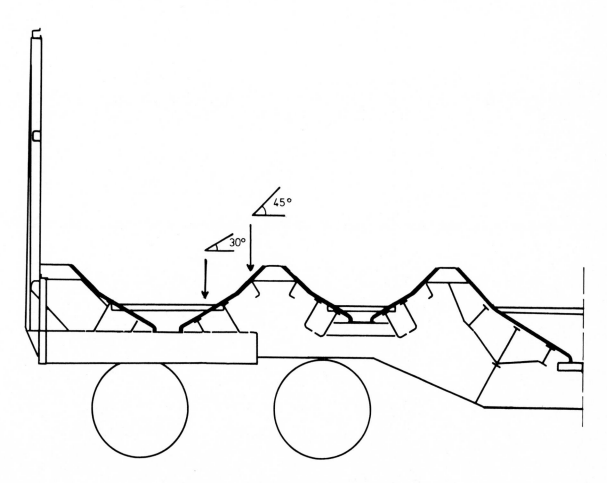

Fig 8 Guiding device for the coils

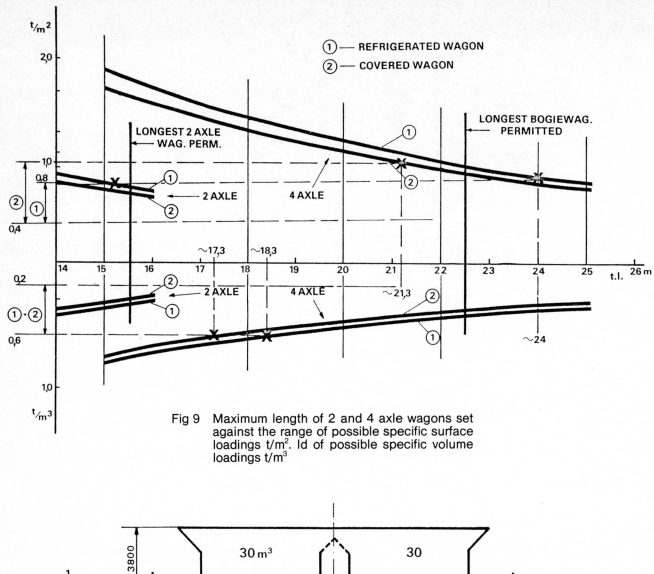

Fig 9 Maximum length of 2 and 4 axle wagons set against the range of possible specific surface loadings t/m². Id of possible specific volume loadings t/m³

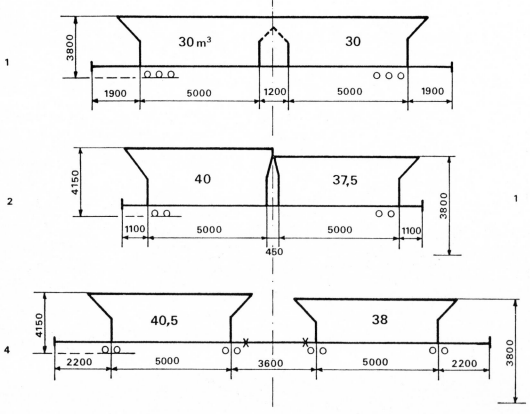

Fig 10 Presentation of one 6 axle, two 4 axle and, two 8 axle self-discharging wagons

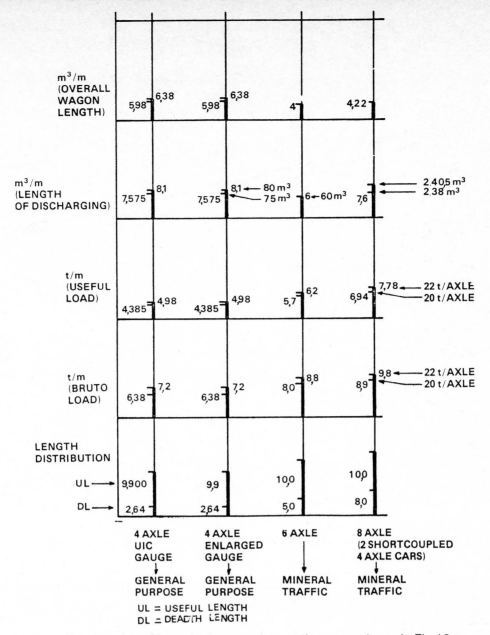

Fig 11   Presentation of important parameters of the wagon types in Fig 10

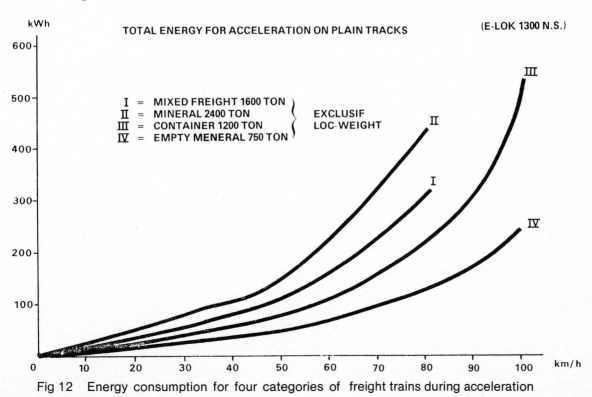

Fig 12   Energy consumption for four categories of freight trains during acceleration

C36/81

Economy of light weight design of vehicles in bulk transportation

J ZEHNDER, Dip Ing ETH
Swiss Aluminium Limited, Zurich, Switzerland

SYNOPSIS   Increasing labour cost and energy prices are incentives for a better evaluation of pros and cons of light weight design of freight wagons for transport of bulk materials.   Although vehicles made in aluminium - coal wagons in the USA, grain hoppers in Canada and Australia, as well as tankers and covered hopper wagons in Europe, have been technically successful, no real breakthrough was achieved: the technical concept did not make full use of the characteristics offered by the relatively young material aluminium and, therefore, the economics of such aluminium wagons showed rather long payback periods.   In order to reduce capital expenditure for aluminium freight wagons, new technologies were developed in recent years. Such concepts are presented and also their commercial value evaluated.

INTRODUCTION

Land transportation of bulk materials is successfully carried out by barges, railroads or road trucks. However, the following will focus on rail transportation only. The oil crisis and the availability of construction materials other than steel have changed the environment of railroads fundamentally and soaring labour costs add to that picture. So, results of investigations about the economics of transportation that were correct a few years ago must now be fundamentally questioned and the evaluation not only updated but completely redone.

Transporation costs

To assess the overall costs for transporting a quantity of material from one point to another is a very complex matter. One must consider the loading and unloading operation at the terminals, the direct labour for shunting and train operation, the indirect labour for in-route control and planning, the investment for track, rolling stock and auxiliaries like stations, repair shops etc., wear of fixed installations and rolling stock as well as energy consumption. Most of these factors are very difficult to attribute to one transportation task. Furthermore, they are so strongly dependent on local conditions that in the following only capital expenditure for rolling stock and energy cost for transportation are considered. It is obvious that such a simplification can influence the conclusions - in favour of traditional heavy rolling stock.

Methods of light weight design

It is evident that light weight rolling stock helps saving energy. That is why ever since rail vehicles have been built, designers tended to make them as light as possible at reasonable costs. Basically, two philosophies can be applied for that purpose:

a) the use of light materials

b) the full utilization of material properties through sophisticated design and manufacturing techniques

Traditionally, steel has been used for manufacturing freight wagons. Lighter materials such as aluminium or glassfibre-reinforced plastics are considerably more expensive. The same is true for high strength steel such as low-alloy high tensile steel or stainless steel. The more sophisticated design calls for a higher labour content to produce the vehicle. Both ways have so far proven successful for designing and manufacturing passenger coaches, especially for use in underground and suburban services, but only to a very limited extent for the design of freight cars. Here, operating conditions are so unfavourable that a wagon of sophisticated design, which is good for normal use, can get badly damaged through misuse and is, therefore, prone to frequent and heavy repair. The use of light weight materials was limited to restricted numbers of vehicles, which, although successful, could not compete with traditional steel wagons.

Traditional aluminium wagons

This is the moment to introduce a selection of light weight freight wagons made in aluminium. The greatest number and variety exists in the family of hopper wagons. The oldest ones were built more than forty years ago in a riveted design, using mainly sheet material and a few standard sections such as L U T Z I, etc. as stiffeners. It is evident that the cost of such a wagon is higher than that of an equivalent steel vehicle, by as much as the cost differential between the raw materials needed for manufacturing, i.e. for a 80 t gross weight hopper wagon in today's money:

6000 kg at £ 1.65 = £ 10 000   aluminium

12000 kg at £ 0.25 = £ 3 000.   steel
    _____

Extra cost: £ 7 000

Amortization of this extra cost within a reasonable period of time was possible only under special conditions, like e.g. very high utilization, unfavourable route conditions i.e. steep gradient, etc. Wagons of that type were in service in Germany, France, the United States, Australia and Morocco.

Next step was the development of welded designs in aluminium, which closely resembled the steel designs of that period. When for the sheet material non-heat treatable alloys were chosen, and for the extrusions either standard heat treatable or non-heat treatable alloys, then, usually, the underframe was made in steel. When using self-hardening alloys, the whole car was made of aluminium. The economic situation of this type of wagons hardly differed from that of riveted ones. Nevertheless, a greater number of such wagons was built all over the world, in the United States, Canada, France, Germany, Switzerland, Australia, Morocco and Rhodesia.

In the same family, we also find a certain number of tank wagons. Here, safety standards do not allow for substantial weight savings. So, from the economic point of view it is even more difficult to justify these vehicles, though they are technically interesting.

New aluminium vehicles

After a long period of research in the field of alloy composition, extrusion technology and manufacturing techniques, a new design concept for rail vehicles is ready for application. This concept has already proven successful for passenger rolling stock: some 3000 underground, suburban and Inter-City coaches are already in service or on order.

The backbone of this concept is the broad use of large extrusions running full length of the wagon. Each extrusion is specially designed for its application, with special emphasis on ingenious joints between extrusions. Transversal stiffeners can to a great extent be dispensed with. Thus, a wagon can be assembled in less time and the cost differential between the raw materials can be compensated to a great extent. It is e.g. possible to obtain extrusions up to 600 mm wide containing integral stiffeners, clamping edges, weld bevel on both edges, backing bar for easy welding and nose and groove system for aligning purposes. Manufacture of a thin

gauge, well-reinforced wall is so brought down to simply carrying out a certain number of continuous welds, preferably automatic welds. The clamping edges can even be designed in such a way that clamping of a wall can be done from one side, leaving the other side free to carry out the welds simultaneously, e.g. with a gantry type multitorch welding machine. On a production basis, the sidewall of a coal wagon measuring 15 by 3 metres can be manufactured in only three to four labour hours. In the prototype stage, with no automatic welding equipment or any jig, 16 manhours were required. It must be mentioned here that the detail design of the extrusion edge needs a lot of experience in order to avoid manufacturing problems arising in connection with clamping in jigs, welding machine setting and, especially, warping due to shrinkage of the weld seams.

Another key factor in the new design is the extrusion holding the automatic coupler. In traditional design, a so-called centre sill or stub sill in the form of two Z sections is welded together to form an Ω shape. The draft gears located at each end of this beam transmit the longitudinal forces acting in the train via front and back stops - usually forgings or castings - which are either welded or riveted to that beam. In the new design, two hollow sections replace both, Z sections and stops. The housing for the draftgear is obtained by milling out on a short length a portion of the material of this special section (Figure 1). Thus, security can be improved and, at the same time, labour saved.

Where sheet material is used, care has been taken that for assembling all sheets are held in grooves of the adjacent profiles so that tack welding is not needed. And finally, most of the beams susceptible to serve as fixations for auxiliary equipment are provided with special slots to receive the respective boltheads without any extra labour, like drilling or welding of bits and pieces (Figure 2).

So far, two different prototype wagons have been manufactured according to that technology, one for 3'6" gauge, the other one for standard gauge but 30 t axle load (Figure 3). Interpolating now for European conditions, with such a coal gondola a weight saving of 6 t, from 23 t to 17 t, can be expected, increasing the payload from 57 t to 63 t, or an increase of 10 %. This improvement goes along with a higher initial cost for that wagon (Table). The equivalent quantity of new aluminium wagons to replace one steel wagon will, according to that estimation, cost £ 23 500. To make up for the extra cost of £ 1 100, the user must get savings in operation. In unit load trains, such a wagon will usually run more than 100 000 km per year, saving no more than 600 000 gross ton km. Sources within BR indicate that the energy consumption for producing 1 gtkm is equal to 0.07 kWh, or, the annual savings per wagon will be more than 40 000 kWh, or about £ 1 000. In other words, tne payback period for the extra investment for the aluminium wagon is slightly over one year.

Table

Cost comparison for Gondola wagons

	Steel wagon	Traditional aluminium wagon	New aluminium wagon
Body weight (t)	12	6	6
Material cost (£)	3000	10000	11000
Labour cost (£)	7500	7500	3000
Cost of bogies, brakes, etc.	12000	12000	12000
Total cost (£)	22500	29500	26000
Relative cost	100 %	131 %	116 %
Relative cost per ton payload	100 %	119 %	105 %

Outlook

Technically speaking, the aluminium wagons for hauling coal, grain, plastic granulates, etc. were successful. Unfortunately, from the economic point of view, this was only true under certain operating conditions. The new concept of large extrusion technology has brought a fundamental change in that respect, reducing the payback period for the extra investment - thanks to light weight design - to approx. one year. Service experience with two different prototypes has so far been satisfactory and preparation for mass production is under way. Especially in countries with rich mineral resources, there is great interest for the new technology and so it is likely that after a reasonable testing period, large scale production will start. Development of other types of bulk commodity wagons will run parallel.

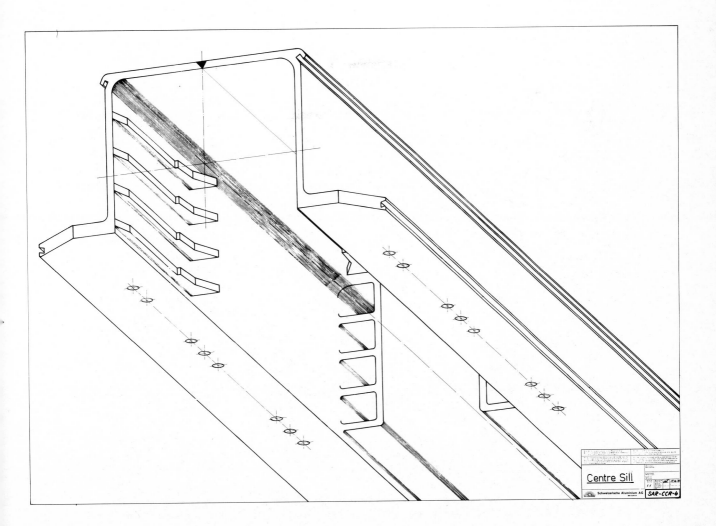

Fig 1   Draft gear housing machined in centre sill section

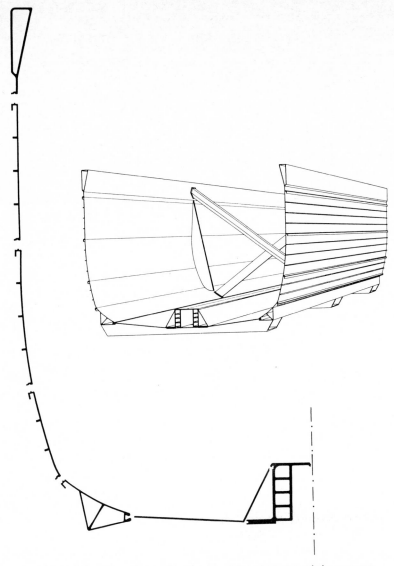

Fig 2   Cross section of a large extrusion gondola wagon

Fig 3   Coal gondola for 30 t axle load

C31/81

Rail freight — future possibilities

R W SPARROW, BA, BAI, PhD, CEng, MICE
British Railways Board, Railway Technical Centre, Derby

SYNOPSIS   A review of future rail freight operating and technical possibilities covering vehicles, dual mode systems, container transfer devices and infra-structure and information technology developments which could improve rail's competitive position.

INTRODUCTION

The freight market is highly competitive; for there to be a healthy rail freight business in the future both efficiency and quality of service must be continually improved. Improvement in efficiency to reduce operating costs requires increased utilisation of equipment and infra-structure and higher productivity from manpower. Reliability and flexibility are key factors in capturing and maintaining market share.

Both operating and technical developments and innovations are necessary to meet these requirements. They must be aimed at minimising the inherent disadvantages of rail transport of high fixed costs and inbuilt system rigidity and exploiting fully rail transport's energy efficiency and low movement costs for large regular flows.

This paper considers the future market and the competition and reviews possible future developments. These include improvements in vehicle suspensions to reduce track damage and wheel wear and the possible use of plastics and light alloys to reduce vehicle weight and maintenance costs. Novel intermodal systems including container transfer devices and methods of operating to improve system coverage and economics will be described. Reference will also be made to infra-structure developments and information technology developments which could reduce costs, and improve operating efficiency. These operational and technical improvements should maintain rail's competitive position and could provide opportunities for future rail freight expansion.

FUTURE MARKET AND COMPETITION

Freight transport is essentially a service industry and as such is highly dependent on the demands which industry at large places on it. Changes in the national economy and in the nature and location of industry and its customers must be considered in forecasting future freight transport requirements. It is also essential to assess the likely response of competing transport operators to these requirements and their developments.

A recent report by TRRL reviews (Ref. 1) trends over past years, and predicts future developments. It confirms that road transport dominates the UK freight market.

There has been a continuing shift to larger road vehicles and these vehicles have been involved in increased lengths of haul. Road vehicle operating costs have been increasing in real terms and this trend is likely to continue. However, the energy efficiency of lorries will increase both from improvements in the prime mover and in the aerodynamics of the vehicle.

Liquid fuels will continue to be used for the foreseeable future. Security of supply is more important than price and industry could well consider alternative transport modes if fuel supplies become uncertain. The effect of fuel prices on the total demand for freight transport is likely to be slight but transport costs will increase.

Freight transport is increasingly being regarded as a component of a total distribution strategy including production, storage, distribution and sales. Decisions which minimise total distribution costs may lead to the acceptance of increased freight transport costs.

Bulk transport represents 90% of rail freight traffic and is confined to a few large industries. The future level of traffic is therefore highly dependent on the future of these industries. It is unlikely that there will be any significant growth in bulk freight except coal and aggregates. Coal traffic is likely to become increasingly important as North Sea oil production declines, and aggregates, as gravel deposits are depleted.

Port traffic is important in total tonnage and is increasing. Containerisation and Ro-Ro traffic on the short sea routes have created significant flows through the South and East coast ports. In 1977 container traffic (Ref. 2) through the UK ports totalled 17 million tonnes and Ro-Ro 16 million tonnes. Both are likely to continue growing.

POSSIBLE TECHNICAL AND OPERATING DEVELOPMENTS IN BULK FREIGHT

Rail freight has been successful in maintaining its share of bulk transport. Operating efficiency has steadily improved with increase in axle load, train size, adoption of rapid loading and discharge facilities and the minimisation of marshalling.

It seems unlikely that any further increase in axle load above 25 tonnes will take place. The civil engineering implications are severe and any increase over 25 tonnes would produce an increase of track maintenance cost out of proportion. It is also unlikely that train size will increase significantly. There are signalling, track layout and terminal limitations which would impose economic penalties. Vehicle improvements, however, to reduce aerodynamic drag, to reduce tare weight or increase capacity, could increase operating efficiency.

The number of collieries and power stations equipped for rapid loading and discharge will increase. Experiments have been completed on the remote control of MGR trains when passing through CEGB hopper houses. This equipment permits the hopper house superintendent to start and stop trains remotely when the locomotive is running under slow speed control. Useful manpower savings result as it is no longer necessary to provide stand-by crews.

A simple device has been developed to allow remote brake continuity testing avoiding the need for train crewmen to walk the length of the train and thus saving time in reversing trains. The device (Fig. 1) consists of a valve which is coupled to the brake pipes at the rear of the train. A piston in the valve held closed by the main reservoir pressure seals the brake pipe. Venting the main reservoir pipe at the front end of the train releases the piston and vents the brake pipe to atmosphere giving the driver an indication of pressure loss as required and proving brake pipe and main reservoir pipe continuity.

Improvements in vehicle technology should increase reliability and reduce maintenance costs. Coil springs or low friction two stage leaf springs will be used for two axle suspensions with controlled yaw stiffness to give improved curving and reduce wheel and rail wear. Bogie suspensions will probably incorporate cross bracing between wheelsets to give good curving performance and stability with fully worn wheel profiles, thus reducing contact stresses between wheel and rail and extending rail life or allowing higher vehicle speed.

A quarter to a third of the weight of a typical freight train represents dead weight. This influences locomotive rating, train capacity, and energy consumption, brake duties and track deterioration. Any weight reduction which could be achieved would benefit one or more of these factors. Improved methods of design and better knowledge of material performance such as fatigue resistance should reduce weight. Similarly,

alternative materials to steel such as light alloys or plastics could also reduce weight. In addition they are corrosion resistant and do not require painting. Although the basic costs of these materials are higher than steel, alternative manufacturing methods possible with these materials can compensate for the extra costs.

POSSIBLE TECHNICAL AND OPERATING DEVELOPMENTS IN GENERAL MERCHANDISE

The most important steps taken by BR to improve performance in the general merchandise sector were the introduction of the Freightliner system, the adoption of the TOPS computer based wagon information and control system and the progressive build up of the Speedlink air braked wagon network.

The Speedlink system is essentially a private siding to private siding operation with a minimum of intermediate marshalling of sectional working. There are comparatively few origins and destinations, the network being coarse and national coverage is therefore limited. The market is selected to suit these system characteristics.

Freightliner is a dual mode system with at least one road transit. Whilst growth in maritime traffic, particularly deep sea, has been healthy, the domestic container traffic has been disappointing, but this largely reflects the economic conditions in recent years. Because the intermodal transfer costs and the collection and delivery costs are a high proportion of total costs, longer distance hauls are favoured and the system is not always economic for short hauls say under 300 km.

Wagon utilisation and turnround are key factors in the overall economics of both Speedlink and Freightliner. Detachable swop bodies or containers are one method of achieving high utilisation of the railway wagon and increasing wagon flexibility to deal with a variety of commodities. Surprisingly the costs per unit of load or per unit of volume available are less for a pair of ISO containers and a Freightliner wagon than for a COV AB. This suggests that even if the containers are not demounted this could be a flexible solution for private siding traffic. Development of low cost container transfer equipment could encourage still greater use of containers in private sidings traffic.

If a significant increase in general merchandise carried by rail is to be achieved, technical and operating developments are required to overcome the present limitations of both Speedlink and Freightliner. Ideally door to door capability is desired. This implies a dual mode system with an element of road haulage and intermodal transfer.

Over the years many dual mode systems have been considered. The simplest in concept is piggy-back where a complete road vehicle or semi-trailer is carried on a rail wagon. This system has been relatively successful in the USA with its large loading gauge and long transcontinental hauls of 1500 km or more. Unfortunately the British loading gauge is extremely restrictive and in general hauls are relatively much shorter. Even with special purpose wagons of the type developed in Austria and Germany only a road semi-trailer of limited height could be carried on BR. The costs of opening out the BR loading gauge would be completely prohibitive and in any event the operating costs do not compare favourably with a container train because of the poor payload and poor aerodynamic characteristics of piggy-back.

Various forms of dual mode vehicle have been proposed, basically road semi-trailers with rail running gear which can be brought into use for the rail haul. The Chesapeake and Ohio railway introduced the 'Rail van' which ran more or less successfully for ten years. A British version 'Roadrailer' (Fig. 2) was manufactured by the Pressed Steel Co. Ltd. in 1960. Technical difficulties and the advent of the 'Linertrain' system caused it to be abandoned. Variants of this basic theme have subsequently been suggested. 'Tracker' (Fig. 3) to overcome the articulation limitation by using two rail wheelsets and 'Trailerail' (Fig. 4) to overcome payload limitations by using detachable articulation bogies. Operational and economic studies, however, showed no significant advantage over the Freightliner system.

A fundamental requirement for significant growth of any general merchandise system is a network capability. Thus only if a new system could show large cost advantages over Freightliner could it be considered as a viable alternative as the Freightliner network already exists. No such system has yet been identified. Ideally, therefore, developments are required which will improve Freightliner economics and extend its network coverage at minimal investment cost whilst generating new traffic.

The most critical costs in Freightliner operation are transfer costs and C & D costs. Detailed studies of alternative container transfer technologies applied to typical large and medium Freightliner terminals showed that a number of novel container handling concepts appeared to offer potential for lower costs. The two most promising concepts were 'Hitch and Switch' and the 'Container Transfer Vehicle'. In the Hitch and Switch concept (Fig. 5) the motion of the container carrying vehicle, either road or rail, is used to elevate the container off the vehicle and onto four supporting legs through a suitable mechanical linkage. The vehicle then draws out from under the container. To load the container onto a vehicle the process is reversed. The concept is currently at the feasibility stage. It l s the potential for very rapid turnround as several vehicles can be loaded or unloaded simultaneously, there are however a number of technical problems yet to be solved.

The Container Transfer Vehicle concept (Fig. 6) is a self powered bogie rail vehicle equipped with a side transfer mechanism to permit lateral transfer of containers from stillage, road vehicles or rail vehicles onto itself and vice versa. It may combine a lifting mechanism to free containers from their twist locks or alternatively, powered self elevating twist locks can be fitted to the rail vehicles.

A very promising form of lifting and transfer mechanism has been proposed for a 'Self Loading Road Vehicle' (Fig. 7) which could be applied to the Container Transfer Vehicle concept. In its road vehicle form it is limited by axle load consideration to a maximum container size of twenty tonnes. This restriction would not apply to a rail mounted mechanism. The initial tilt required subjects the container to no greater lateral acceleration than would be experienced by negotiating road roundabouts.

These concepts offer the possibility of low cost enhancements to existing terminals to increase throughput or to introduce new terminals into the network at minimum cost. The Container Transfer Vehicle and Self Loading Road Vehicle are to be taken further to the experimental prototype stage.

Computer based simulation techniques have been developed to enable terminal operations to be studied in considerable depth, for example for planning purposes to achieve optimum choice of handling equipment and terminal layout and for real time applications to day-to-day terminal management. These techniques have been applied to the C & D operation for scheduling purposes with considerable promise. It seems quite feasible to use computers for assisting with all the planning and monitoring activities carried out by the cartage office and to produce planning schedules and container movement instructions and documentation.

Whilst computer assistance can improve the C & D operation the only fundamental way of substantially reducing costs of this operation is to reduce the radius of operation. This implies an increase in the number of terminals and requires re-consideration of the method of operation of the rail haul between terminals to maximise train loading. Currently two methods of maximising train loading are used: 'Section working' whereby Freightliner trains call at a number of terminals en route exchanging containers or wagon sets. The other method is 'link traffic' in which containers are routed between origins and destinations via one or more intermediate terminals from which a direct service is operated. Neither method readily provides an economic 'any terminal to any terminal' service which is desirable to maximise market capture.

A possible solution is to re-consider the use of sorting centres. In classic wagon load operation this was the prime function of the marshalling yard. This is by no means a novel proposal and was suggested as long ago as 1910 by Mr A.W. Gattie. Indeed his proposal (Ref. 3) for a clearing house in London using unitised loading and fully mechanised handling was far ahead of its time.

A modern version of this proposal merits serious consideration. A feasibility study has therefore been completed by the R & D Division of the use of a single national container sorting centre as a hypothetical limiting case. This took as its starting point an estimate of the total Freightliner domestic market and a full matrix of all current container terminal flows.

The feasibility study showed that, theoretically, savings in container transit costs could be made and that the wagon fleet could be reduced. It also eliminated the need for section working or link traffic and achieved an 'any terminal to any terminal' capability. It made the case for setting up new terminals more attractive and would probably generate new traffic.

In view of the apparent potential of this hypothetical limiting case further studies are currently in hand to determine the optimum use that could be made of some existing terminals as sorting centres. Initial findings are very encouraging.

If this form of operation could be combined with additional low cost terminals using transfer equipment of the type referred to earlier it should be possible to stimulate growth of traffic with modest investment.

Developments currently in hand in vehicle technology are aimed at producing Freightliner wagons of greater reliability and longer life with minimal maintenance. A novel form of welded underframe 'Convex' (Fig. 8) removes the welds from highly stressed locations and reduces the cost of fabrication. If this concept proves successful in the prototype tests about to begin it could become the standard future Freightliner underframe. Bogie developments referred to earlier particularly aimed at reducing maintenance costs and track damage could also help to improve performance and perhaps allow higher running speeds, thus simplifying pathing problems.

Thus all the elements necessary to produce a radical evolution of the Freightliner concept to give a product of considerable potential in the general merchandise sector are likely to become available. Given modest levels of investment it would seem possible to increase rail's share of this very large market. Whilst perhaps on a national level this would not greatly alter the balance of the market between road and rail nevertheless the importance to BR of such an increase in freight traffic would be considerable.

CROSS CHANNEL RAIL LINK

As mentioned earlier cross channel traffic into Europe is a growth area. Rail's competitive position could be considerably improved by further moves to containerisation, the introduction of jumbo train ferries or by the construction of a rail only Channel Tunnel. In the latter case it is estimated that some 7.9 million tonnes of freight could be carried through the tunnel by the year 2000. International container traffic by rail would then be extremely competitive with road and should increase. In the meantime the introduction of 100 wagon jumbo train ferries would transform the economics of train ferry operation and might add 1.5 million tonnes a year to the Speedlink business.

OTHER FUTURE DEVELOPMENTS OF SIGNIFICANCE TO RAIL FREIGHT

Developments not directly concerned with freight technology but which nevertheless could be of significance are aimed at reducing railway infra-structure costs and improving communications.

Two such developments on track are the establishment of numerical track roughness standards for secondary passenger and freight lines and the development of new forms of track maintenance machine. The use of track recording cars and the availability of numerical standards of track roughness should provide the civil engineers with means of controlling track maintenance more precisely in the future and hence reduce costs. A new form of track maintenance machine is under development intended to replace tamping machines used for lining and levelling track. Instead of disturbing the ballast under the sleepers to pack the sleepers to the required level, additional stone is introduced between the sleeper and the stable ballast bed pneumatically. It has been shown in trials that the maintenance cycle can be lengthened considerably with major potential cost savings.

Developments in signalling are aimed at reducing costs by replacing bulky and costly electro-mechanical relay interlockings with microprocessors. For lightly used lines the replacement of pole routes, cabling, and signalling by radio communication can produce cost savings. In addition, should traffic requirements change in the future the equipment can be readily transferred, thus increasing flexibility, and avoiding abortive investment. The use of radio is likely to increase rapidly in the future. Development of microprocessor controlled transmitters and receivers are opening up possibilities for low cost application to many fields with economy in the use of the limited range of frequencies allocated to BR by the Home Office.

By combining these developments with others such as automatic wagon and container identification, low cost visual display terminals and facsimile machines and the use of computers for control and scheduling of operations, a management information and control system of great power will emerge.

CONCLUSIONS

The future level of rail freight traffic will be highly dependent on the state of the national economy. Unless there is a marked upturn, only coal and maritime container traffic are likely to show any overall growth. Rail freight will therefore be in an increasingly competitive market with surplus capacity in all modes.

The increased lengths of haul already required by industry, possible uncertainty in future fuel supplies, and increase in real costs of road transport, despite off-setting improvements in performance of vehicles and prime movers, should assist rail's competitive position.

Freight transport will increasingly be considered as only one component of complete physical distribution strategy by industry and specialist transport operators. There could be opportunities for rail transport either alone or in partnership in this field.

Technical improvements in rail vehicle design to increase reliability, to reduce weight, to reduce maintenance costs and to reduce aerodynamic drag will improve efficiency of operation. Operational methods will be refined and the use of technology such as remote control of trains will improve productivity of equipment and manpower.

In general merchandise no new dual mode or intermodal concepts seem likely to emerge to seriously challenge the potential of the Freightliner concept. A future rail based general merchandise system will probably evolve from the present Freightliner network. The basic elements required for such evolution are already becoming available.

The introduction of jumbo train ferries and the construction of the Channel Tunnel should increase rail's share of traffic into Europe.

Other developments in a wider context to reduce rail infra-structure costs and to improve communications including radio and electronic data processing should assist in improving the overall performance of rail freight operation.

These future developments and possibilities should enable rail freight to retain a key role in the nation's freight transport requirements, and thus contribute to the conservation of energy.

ACKNOWLEDGEMENTS

This paper is published by permission of the British Railways Board but the views expressed are those of the author. It is based on projects and studies carried out by a number of groups and individuals within the Research & Development Division. The bulk of the work, however, was undertaken in the Transport Technology Assessment Group under P.J. Howarth and in the Mechanical Engineering Research Branch under J.R. Mitchell.

REFERENCES

1.   CORCORAN P.J., HITCHCOCK A.J., McMAHON C.M. Developments in Freight Transport TRRL Supplementary Report 580-1980.

2.   Freight Transport - Central Office of Information Reference Pamphlet No. 101-1971.

3.   HORNIMAN R. - How to Make the Railways Pay for the War or The Transport Problem Solved. Published by George Routledge & Son 1919.

Fig 1   Remote brake pipe continuity test valve

Fig 2 Roadtrailer

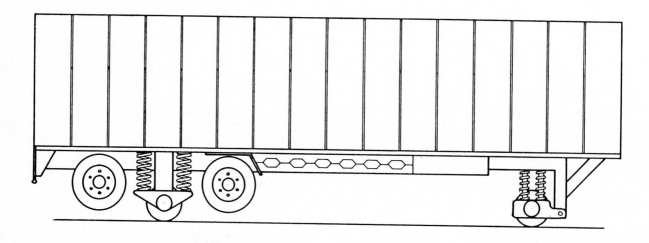

Fig 3 Tracker

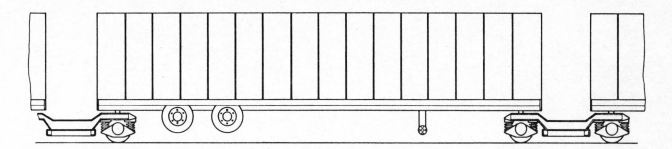

Fig 4   Trailerail

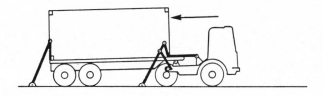

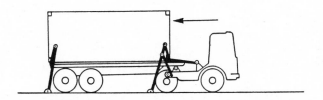

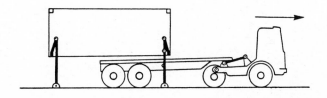

Fig 5   Hitch and switch

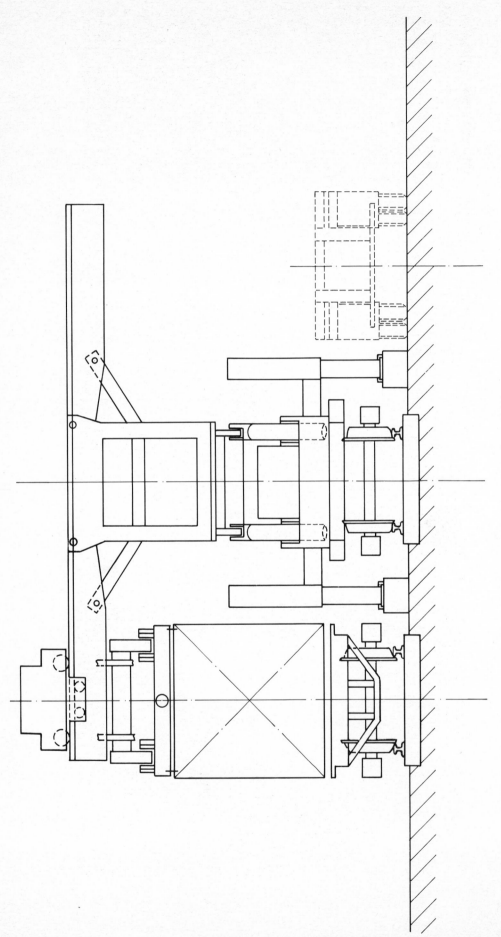

Fig. 6 Container transfer vehicle

Fig 7   Self loading road vehicle: Sequence a
                                                                Sequence b
                                                                Sequence c

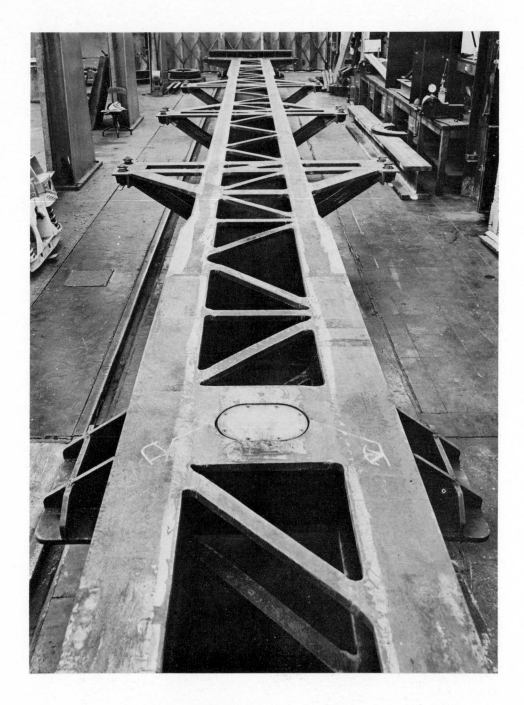

Fig 8   Convex freightliner underframe

C37/81

More rail freight

F J SWINDELL, CEng, MIMechE
Procor (UK) Limited

Rail is the natural means of conveyance for bulk traffic, while at the other end of the scale for local distribution and door to door movements under 150 kilometres, road transport is the natural mode. Between lies the area of real competition and our future.

The Railways have always had to pay the full cost of its infrastructure. Many of the largest lorries which compete with rail freight are not making adequate payments for the use of the road infrastructure which is provided by Local and Central Government. The method of payment, vehicle excise duty and fuel tax ensure that for any group of lorries not paying its way those lorries performing the highest mileages are the ones that receive the largest subsidies. A 32/33 tonne four-axle articulated lorry in 1980, travelling 100 000 miles per annum, pays a total tax revenue of just under £8 000 to support a £12 000 total public attributed road cost - Department of Transport statistic. Unless this tax is increased, there will be a further benefit for the even bigger lorries that are now forecast.

Surely this is an area where public spending could be curtailed by creating legislation where the heavy goods vehicle has to pay fully to support the road infrastructure. The levying of true road taxes on the road haulier would allow the railways to compete fairly. In that scenario, would the Section 8 Grant be as important as it is today?

Full economies between road and rail need examination. Take two types of freight train that operate in the U.K. The large iron-ore train with two Class 56 Loco's with a trailing load of 3 300 tonnes uses 5.7 gallons of fuel per mile where it would take 100 32/33 tonne road lorries using a total fuel consumption of 12.5 gallons per mile. Likewise a smaller 500 tonne aggregate hopper train with a Class 37 Loco has a fuel consumption of 1.07 gallons per mile where 16 road lorries use a total of 2 gallons per mile. Environmentally, everything favours rail, but it is the railways and the private service companies that must create a more commercial approach to winning freight to rail and not by pricing alone but by covering siding

agreements, freight service, reliability, wagon availability, customer service priorities and total management of wagon fleets.

The private side and the railways should have policies and objectives to gain more rail freight.

1. The Railways Board to give more importance to rail freight in all its aspects - bulk train, Speedlink, Freightliner and international traffic.

2. Go for volume - not restrict itself to selected convenient train load and Speedlink movements. Some major customers believe that there is a real danger of allowing the freight business to shrink so small that it could lose significant traffics altogether.

3. Plan more aggressively - create the position of Freight Managing Director to co-ordinate marketing and services and ensure closer relationships with the Regions whose sales executives are the closest to the countrywide opportunities. This would separate the passenger side from the freight business.

   The plan for phasing out B.R. stock over the next decade should be done with the planned replacement of wagons and locomotives.

4. We should make more use of private side resources, both private owners and users, particularly for financing, designing of special purpose wagons, building and repairing. We should also give some consideration to appointing some Private Wagon Federation men to the Regional Boards.

5. Co-ordinate technical and research work to improve the product.

6. Develop the Freightliner business. Freightliners are devoted to the box.

Change is coming. With the move from the 8ft 6in high I.S.O. to a few 9 ft high containers. This will require new designs of low liner or well wagons on pre-selected routes.

Freightliners are well positioned at strategic points in the U.K. Let them also handle specialised wagons in small numbers or single wagon load traffic. Develop their terminals to allow the short-haul road operators or existing B.R. customers access to discharge their own wagons for local distribution.

Developing these objectives, let us look at the 'go for volume'. The exhibition display of wagons shows the modern trend for more specialised wagons. The petroleum and chemical Companies are obvious but to increase their traffic, a fine balance between the total cost of safety against commercial judgement has to be made or traffic will continue to move by other modes. Grain, powders and aggregates also command highly specialised wagons but the opportunities for foodstuffs, motor-cars, car components, commercial vehicle carriers, Ministry of Defence, milk tankers, scrap etc., are some of the areas for the good design and cleverly priced haulage rates can be captured back from the road haulier.

Using the same type of standard rail van for a commodity like Cornflakes and tin plate is not good enough. B.R. Marketing and the Designers must work on this type of problem together.

There needs to be co-ordination of technical and research work. Building wagons today, we use the standard B.R. criteria and recommendations. This produces wagons with a minimum tare of around the 12 tonne mark for four wheeler and a minimum 23 tonnes for bogie vehicles, physically committing ourselves to steel wagon designs. Larger capacity, lighter tare, means the use of aluminium or plastics with steel.

The recommendations today give little design guidance in terms of fatigue. No fatigue loads are provided and no recommended fatigue method. The designer has to judge what the fatigue load might be and then suggest a sensible design method. Let us say that we build with steel frames and aluminium barrels. The joint between the aluminium and steel which would be combined in a member to react buckling loads. Steel would be carrying most of the load anyway. You cannot do it so easily on an aluminium vehicle. You need a design method to use the aluminium/plastic part sensibly in calculations. You should do failure modes and effects analyses in calculations - the reason why things fail. Design modes for resonance buckling fatigue also should include creep. Plastics creep at 100° - 200°C. Some of this criteria is operational with the German Federal Railways. The U.I.C. should also reflect these requirements to move to total European Standards for our railways.

Lighter tares will create suspension and brake problems. We should plan for extended trials with the B.R. Research for suspensions and brakes for brake development to cope with the gap between the light tare and the total permissible gross laden weight. A good example of such a unit, which will go on trial, is the Procam combined brake and suspension unit (Patent pending). This invention relates to braking systems for rail freight wagons.

There are two basic types of braking systems which have been used for rail freight wagons. The first system uses clasp brakes, which consist of beams suspended on hangers from the frame. Blocks are fitted to the ends of the beams and the blocks are applied through a system of levers, rods, slack adjuster and an air cylinder all mounted on the vehicle body. The second system uses disc brakes, where disc plates are attached to the wagon wheels and pads are actuated through calipers, and a combined slack adjuster unit and air cylinder all mounted from the vehicle body. The disc brake system is a more recent development and a large proportion of wagons built over recent years have been fitted with one disc per axle giving a substantial weight and space advantage because all the brake gear is confined to the outboard ends of the wagon and no brake beams are used, allowing for hoppers or other equipment to come very close to the axles.

Recently service problems have developed with disc brakes in certain operating conditions. The result is that on 60 mph operation and 25 tonne axle loads it is usually necessary to fit two discs per axle on new vehicles, substantially increasing the building costs.

Over the years, new brake blocks have been developed to replace cast iron blocks for conventional clasp brakes. Cast iron is heavy, quick wearing, produces metallic dust and can be a fire hazard due to heat or sparking. Most of the new blocks are the high friction composition (h.f.c.) type, they are extremely light and have a co-efficient of friction approximately twice that of cast iron. This means the energy required to operate the blocks is half that of a comparable cast iron system.

The development of lightweight low pressure blocks has helped another type of tread braking system, that of an axle-mounted clasp brake. On this system the entire braking system is mounted from the casing of the wheel bearing. Brake arms are pivoted from extensions of the bearing casing. Blocks are positioned part-way up the arms and the blocks are applied to the wheel by pulling the tops of the arms together. This system provides extreme lightweight, compact design, an exact relationship of wheel and block regardless of suspension travel. The last feature is very desirable for handbrake operation as well as block performance.

C37/81

It is the object of this invention to provide an integrated suspension and brake package with the following special features:

1. An arrangement that uses the minimum amount of space. The actuator is mounted at the side of the brake arm and between the suspension and the wheel. On a two axle wagon this provides the maximum load space. The actuator is also below the top of the wheel flange, this enables one design to be also used on primary suspension bogie wagons. In this position, the actuator, a proprietary hydraulic slave cylinder, is also protected from thermal damage and debris thrown from the wheel. The brake block is mounted on the opposite side of a tubular brake arm to the actuator to balance out some of the torque reaction.

2. A slack adjuster that has only one moving part, its friction surfaces are non-metallic and therefore not affected by corrosion, and it is easy to assemble having no keys, springs or dowels. A boss is provided at each end of the suspension saddle casting. A boss is drilled and fitted with a simple pin. The pin has an interference fit through the boss and is threaded at the end. Friction material is bonded either side of a thick rubber disc and to a face of the boss and to a face on the brake arm. The brake arm, which is bushed, and the rubber discs are mounted on the pin so that the friction surfaces make contact. A nut holds the arm on the pin and compresses the rubber to a pre-determined amount. The assembly can take place with the arm in any position. Pushing the blocks towards the wheel provides a twist/slip action at the pivot. The block having a spring return action. This device provides a running clearance at the block it also acts as a shock absorber to the bearing, also non-metallic, in the brake arm and it is not affected by corrosion or high wear because of the small incremental movement involved.

3. Brake block attachment method that uses existing designs of block but which can withstand the high shock loads from the wheelset, and uses a similar method of locking to that already used within the industry. On conventional clasp brakes the block is a loose fit in the brake block back. The block is retained by a rough forged brake key. The key is prevented from coming out, although not coming loose, by a split pin near the bottom end of the key. In this invention, a specially fabricated and pivotted brake block retains the block accurately. The block is held by driving in a precision shallow taper key (standard UIC part). Before the key is driven home it rubs against a simple keeper plate, that is also designed as a guide when locating the key. When the key is in the correct position a hole in the key aligns with a hole on the keeper plate and the conventional split pin retains the key. There are other holes further down the plate in the event of wear taking place. During manufacture of the brake block back a dummy block and key are used to determine the position of the keeper plate holes.

4. A handbrake system that, like the power brake, is hydraulically operated but locks on mechanically. On one power brake system in four a hand-brake actuator is fitted. The unit is a modified proprietary item and acts like a simple hydraulic cylinder except the pushrod passes through a one way clutch and locks the handbrake on mechanically. Hydraulic pressure to the clutch releases the brake. The power brake slave cylinder pushrod and the parking brake actuator pushrods are connected. If none of the lines to the parking brake actuator are pressurised its pushrod is free to move, and the power brake automatically adjusts it. The development and testing of this brake is a good example where the private side and railway Research will work closely together in the proving trials.

The power to plan more aggressively has to be looked at with the British Rail fleet standing today at 125 000 wagons. The forecast is 31 000 by 1990 and half of those will be merry-go-round coal wagons. Both sides of the industry should now be planning for the wagons of the future so that the phasing out of the old stock takes place as the new larger capacity, lighter tared wagons enter traffic. Knowledge by designers, builders and financiers of planned withdrawals can avoid indulgence in generalised guesswork about the replacements and the types of special-ised vehicles. We should pay more attention to tailoring the wagons to suit the traffic and wherever possible create long term contracts for base annual loads giving security to both B.R., user and supplier.

The present phasing out of the old stone carrying vehicles, both box car and hoppers, and the replacement by the new 50 tonne car for aggregates, has worked well over the last few years by B.R. introducing competition for the supply of vehicles to the aggregate Companies. As the B.R. fleet retirement accelerates and indeed the private side fleet which also has a large number of small payload, heavy-tared, vacuum-braked wagons, all of which will need replacement or refurbishing in the next decade. The key must be in sensible planning. The railways should create incentives in their haulage rates to encourage the present private owner to accelerate modernisation by expanding the use of certain haulage contracts which have been introduced so that the customer pays purely for the gross weight of the train. An excellent example is the Phillips Petroleum

100 tonne gross weight vehicle performing up to 80,000 miles per annum with a tare weight of 23 tonnes and a payload of 22 000 imperial gallons, the largest operating in Europe.

If this existing fleet is replaced by capacity, and B.R. also go for volume in the market-place, not only is the major wagon building and funding to plan for but the state of the locomotive fleet today will not cope. Firstly, the ruling on the borrowing ceilings for the Board will not allow this expansion to give an efficient air-braked freight network, so a new fleet of purpose-built locomotives is badly needed. How can this be paid for? This is unlikely in today's economic climate of cut-backs that Treasury ceilings would be increased, but I would suggest that pressure should be brought to bear to allow the British Railways Board to fund money in the City, where there is security, the basic requirement for financing. Of all the major companies that move products in bulk, a large percentage of them have ten year contracts with B.R. and new ten year contracts are being written today. There is no provision in that contract to guarantee locomotive availability and when the economy starts to move there will be frustrations because of locomotive shortages. Therefore, when the Railways undertake a ten year contract, could they not give a guarantee of locomotive availability where the locomotive could be paid for out of the revenues earned on that haulage. This does not necessarily mean that particular flows would have captive locomotives but just a guarantee of availability. That would allow the Railways to organise and build new locomotives in the best manner and pay for them from revenue. These locomotives would be funded from the private financial institutions. Wagon hirers have shown interest in supplying funds and certainly the major banks would be interested if there was a guarantee of service from major oil Companies, chemical companies, aggregate companies etc. creating an actual lean on the B.R. contract.

Finally, the people in the industry motivating each other to achieve some hard nosed objectives and by bringing a more concerted effort in the political field that freight will survive. We have it within our total resources to get more freight on rail. Britain as a nation needs its railway and the development of freight as a first-class service must be done.

The Inland Freight Market 1978 Shares

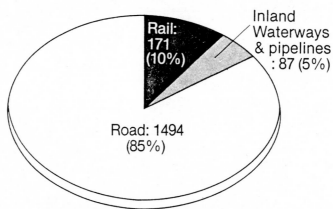

Rail: 171 (10%)

Inland Waterways & pipelines : 87 (5%)

Road: 1494 (85%)

Tonnes (m) Total: 1752 million tonnes

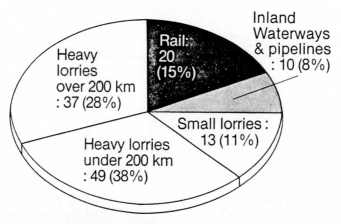

Heavy lorries over 200 km : 37 (28%)

Rail: 20 (15%)

Inland Waterways & pipelines : 10 (8%)

Small lorries : 13 (11%)

Heavy lorries under 200 km : 49 (38%)

Tonne-Kilometres (000m) Total: 129,000 million tonne-kilometres

Source: DTp Transport Statistics

Fig 1   The inland freight market shares

Fig 2 Renault car transporter

Fig 3 Ribble cement wagon

RAIL BUSINESS REVIEW 1980-1990
WAGON FLEET FORECAST

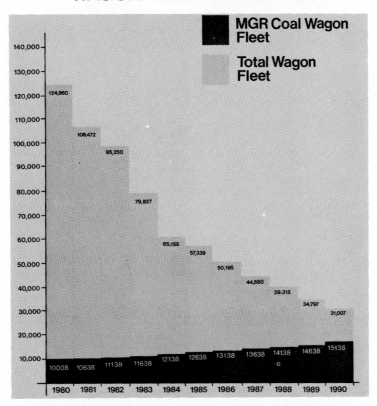

Fig 4 Graph of the British Railway fleet reductions

Fig 5 Foster Yeoman block train of aggregate hoppers

Fig 6   Block train of Phillips petroleum wagons

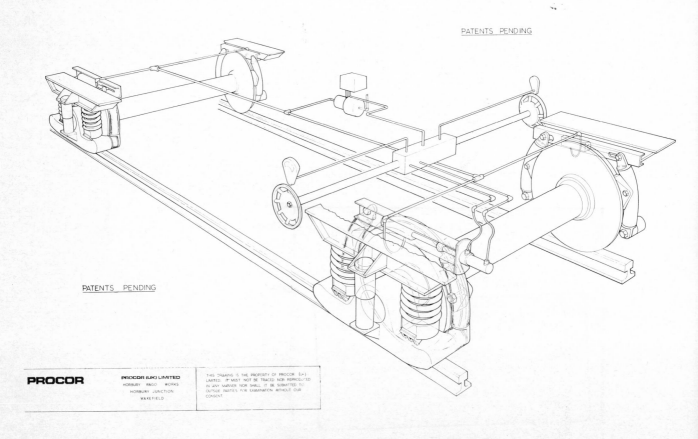

PATENTS PENDING

PATENTS PENDING

Fig 7   Line drawing of the Procam brake

© IMechE 1981   C37/81